Bjarki,

On Floorboards,
Love, and
Irreconcilable
Differences

Not

Bjarki

MATTHEW J. C. CLARK

University of Iowa Press, Iowa City

University of Iowa Press, Iowa City 52242
Copyright © 2023 by Matthew J. C. Clark
uipress.uiowa.edu
Printed in the United States of America

Design by Ashley Muehlbauer

Printed on acid-free paper

Library of Congress Cataloging-in-Publication Data
Names: Clark, Matthew J. C., 1982– author.
Title: Bjarki, Not Bjarki: On Floorboards, Love, and
Irreconcilable Differences / Matthew J. C. Clark.
Description: Iowa City: University of Iowa, 2023.
Identifiers: LCCN 2023015303 (print) | LCCN 2023015304
(ebook) | ISBN 9781609389352 (paperback) |
ISBN 9781609389369 (ebook)
Subjects: LCSH: Clark, Matthew J. C., 1982– | Authors,
American—21st century—Biography. | LCGFT: Essays.
Classification: LCC PS3603.L365325 Z46 2023 (print) |
LCC PS3603.L365325 (ebook) | DDC 813/.6 [B]—dc23/
eng/20230623
LC record available at https://lccn.loc.gov/2023015303
LC ebook record available at https://lccn.loc.gov/2023015304

Contents

For The Wood Mill of Maine

Bjarki, Not Bjarki

ONE

Manatee (Afterward)

Of course, from one perspective, there was no separation. I put on a mask in Maine and a few hours later arrived a breeze away from the warm Atlantic, on the site of a former pineapple plantation, under a magnificent old banyan, at my dear friend J's condo. There were vitamins in the fridge, fruit in the bowl, a gun in the closet. This is how you bring a round into the chamber, how you aim for the kill zone, squeegee the shower, take out the trash. I would be staying at J's for the next few months, but honestly, my mind was elsewhere—is almost always elsewhere—whatever that means. See, that's the trouble with us Aquarians: we're always further away than you. More literal too, B would say. We'd been together for fourteen years, married for eight, which—*eight*—she always said was significant because of something to do with either infinity or nothingness. I mean, there *was* the mileage of The Separation, but like I said, that was nothing.

J would leave in three days. In the time we had together, we spent long hours at the dining room table, working on our respective projects. J was writing a book about dreams in Spanish. Or rather, *first* he was writing the book in English and then he was translating it into Spanish. As a psychological framework, he said, the hero's journey was outmoded. He thought that when he finished the dream book, he'd write another, this one about the *real* Spain, not the Spain that was depicted in a favorite book of mine, which, presumably, wasn't real. There was a chandelier above us, a porcelain toucan in a hutch, lizards on the patio screen. The condo might actually have been J's parents' condo. The floor was tile. J liked to work shirtless, wearing only a small, reversible, mesh swimsuit, and sometimes, without saying anything, he'd stand, place his hands on the terra-cotta, and lift his pale legs into the air, inverting for what felt like several minutes.

My project, conceived four years prior as a magazine-style essay about floorboards, had since swollen into something nearly unrecognizable.

We were out by the pool when I told him.

I said, I've been outsmarted, hoodwinked, bamboozled by a floor.

In fact, though, that's not what I said at all.

The gin and the underwater lights had cleansed us of all delusion.

Reality, J said, is a metaphor for reality.

In other words, I said, a metaphor for reality *is* reality.

While my particular training was in carpentry, I suppose the reason J knew so much about reality and modes and that type of thing was because of his many years in academia and abroad. He was either separated from or separating from or still madly in love with the woman he had lived with or was still living with in Kyiv. Over the years, he'd had several girlfriends from Eastern Europe or Russia, and I was unable to keep their names straight. I knew only that they had all been great in bed and taught J many mysterious things and as a result I was not infrequently jealous. We talked some about me and B too, but mostly I was too confused to talk very long.

In the afternoons, we took J's parents' bicycles to the beach, weaving lazily from shade to sun, from sidewalk to traffic, cursing freely and with gusto the smog-belching pickups, the immaculate green lawns, the houses with old election signs out front. Though it was true that I had many things in my life, clearly there were many people who had many more—*things*, that is. I was nearly thirty-nine years old, riding a friend's mom's cruiser, ringing its little bell, yelling at people I'd never met. You know those clowns at the circus, riding those miniature bikes? It wasn't quite what I'd imagined, though in retrospect, maybe it was better. I loved racing myself over the high bridges into the wind so that I was up there with the osprey looking down, fishing the wide intercoastal and the river. Once, I swear, one of the fishermen crowding the rail pulled up a zebrafish. I mean, I didn't have any idea what kind of fish it was, but it looked like a zebrafish. Or rather, it looked like what I imagined a zebrafish looked like. It was the size of a slim novel and sparkling, striped so definitely, so intentionally, so unbelievably black and white.

You have to be careful with gin, especially when the bottle is blue and you are alone, though sometimes exceptions should be made. Immediately after J left, I made a strong exception, spooned out the ice, and wandered from room to room, pawing through cabinets and drawers, hoping, I think, to find something perverse and illustrative, something that might provide certainty and comfort. I found J's sunscreen, an SPF 70, and put some on. I found his wide-brimmed sun hat and I put that on too. Then I stood before the fridge assembling small magnetic poetry. We will look anywhere, do anything. Honey, tick, kidney, sponge. Out by the pool, a woman sat tending to a jigsaw puzzle. She was the color of a penny. Me—I'm probably the whitest white dude you'll ever see. It's annoying. The world has heaped its fruits upon me, and yet I can only wear certain colors. There were pink flamingos on my blue bathing suit. The water was perfect, buoyant and chilly. Place your warm hand on your cool belly. Does your belly feel the warm or does your hand feel the cool? This, I think, is one of the fundamental mysteries. As I gathered my things, the woman looked up and informed me that my chair was out of line. Of course, I said. I'm so sorry, I said, saying nothing about how the chair wasn't literally *mine*, nor anything about how, with its white vinyl straps, it more aptly resembled a basket, and besides, I did not say, not even the finest instruments of science can return an object to the position it has occupied before, not exactly. I dragged the chair, or whatever it was, loudly, and left it slightly askew. Then I went inside and did not cry. On the counter, seashells filled a vase, which rhymes with *lace* and *jaws*.

A long time ago, my mom gave me this red wool hat with the brim and earflaps and everything. I don't know why I wanted such a specific hat, if I'd just read *The Catcher in the Rye* or what, but Holden Caulfield, he's always putting on or taking off a hat like that, symbolizing something, probably. A big goofy hat, there's a kind of power in it. When I put it on, my whole mood changed, in a good way, though occasionally I felt so silly I became ashamed. It's crazy that a hat can make you feel ashamed, though it's probably not the hat that makes you feel. Though what does *make you feel*? I called it my *wabbit-hunting* hat. I've never hunted anything in my life, and yet, at the same time, I'm always hunting something.

In the mornings, I did yoga. I had only recently initiated this practice because, though B taught yoga in Maine, I hadn't really been into it before The Separation. You can probably see why, but I couldn't tell you why. In particular, I preferred the ministrations of an instructor on YouTube who was both perfectly formed physically and yet not physically attractive at all, traits for which I both resented and admired her. I worked on my abs.

Then I'd bicycle to a coffee shop, which I did not call *a café*, and, under the generous shade of an oak, as the caffeine set in, I would become more and more absorbed in whatever it was I thought I was writing, so much so that I saw nothing beyond my subjects and themes, at least as I understood them then, namely: The Wood Mill of Maine and its owner, Bjarki Thor Gunnarsson—not B—and those pine floorboards that were wider and more American and metaphorical then any pine boards anywhere, except maybe the pine boards in the past and the pine boards in my mind.

It was an SUV, a white one, of course, that hit me, in front of a Walgreens also, it seemed, of course. When I stood up, the driver was trembling and apologetic, as was I, which I'm sure explains why I lied to her, why I said, No worries, I'm fine, never better. And yet, my rear wheel was warped, probably irreparably. I put the wounded bicycle in her trunk and then, back at J's condo, she and I did interplanetary things to each other and swore never to part. I am not speaking euphemistically. It's just that some things take place in other, private dimensions.

Can we finally say that Santa really does exist? I saw him on a roof, straddling an elephant, flying a helicopter. It was 70 degrees in the sun and there she was, ringing a bell in her insulated reds, mask on. A man in Terminix coveralls came to the condo and pointed an aerosol toward hard-to-reach places. Ants, he said. Cockroaches. God, I was afraid of running over a lizard. They were literally—not *literally*—everywhere. Some, I learned later, like the red-headed rock agama, were "non-native," "invasives"—whatever that meant—but anyway, *native* or *non*, they never seemed to move unless I did, flicking at the corner of my vision like the way things might have been, small ones and the biggest too that were nearly the size of squirrels and that I assumed were males, with their neck flaps that flared either to intimidate or to attract other lizards, or maybe to regulate temperature, I wasn't sure. I wanted neck flaps for all of those reasons. I called my therapist. I Zoomed with friends and family. Several times, I talked with B—she was in Maine—about the cat and the virus and how we *needed* to talk seriously about The Separation and then we didn't talk any more about it.

A while back, a couple years ago probably, we'd been sitting on the kitchen steps at Robinson Street—different steps, but not very different. We didn't know why we were coming apart.

I said, "I just want to feel more connected."

B said, "What would that even look like?"

On Christmas, I drank a few exceptions and ate meatless meat—Impossible
—tacos.

On New Year's, the same.

J returned the day before I flew back to Maine. I distinctly remember his
half laugh when he looked up from his phone and said, "They just stormed
the Capitol."

We were sitting in the sand. The ocean was a color I did not have a word
for. I mean, it *was* blue, but blue was leaving out a lot.

Bjarki, the ostensible subject of The Book—he texted me an image of a
tree with the words, THE TREE OF LIBERTY MUST BE REFRESHED FROM
TIME TO TIME WITH THE BLOOD OF PATRIOTS.

Bjarki: I give it a year to 2 years before shit is proper fucked.

Matthew: It's the pine tree!

Bjarki: Ohhh, the symbolism!

Bjarki: Perhaps I'll have to redo The Wood Mill logo

Matthew: Yes!

Matthew: The blood of patriots in your floor!

Bjarki's pretty into politics, which used to drive me nuts, but I don't care
so much about that part of him anymore. I'm trying to focus on my own
patriotism, if I can. It's pronounced *bee-arky*. When I look back on this text
exchange, it is not the flippancy of our tone that stands out to me, but the
fact that the tree in Bjarki's text is definitely deciduous, definitely not, as I
suggested, a pine.

"Seal!" That's me shouting.

J says there are no seals here.

He says, "Look at this clown."

I consider a photograph of a man wearing animal skins.

A raft of seaweed floats past. The seaweed doesn't look like a seal, but it
does look like it could look like a seal. All the waves are breaking at an angle
to the steep beach. In Maine, the sand rolls out flat for the castles and the

seagulls and the lovers. Last summer, just a few miles west of Robinson Street, a great white shark killed a woman. She was swimming in a wetsuit and everybody said that to the shark she must have looked like a seal. The newspaper described horrors. I have always said that I'd rather be eaten alive by a shark than a bear, but that was always hypothetical.

A few years prior, I had come to this very same beach with J. Supposedly, I was on vacation. However, there is no such thing as vacation. However, vacation is still quite nice. I remember the people arriving that afternoon with their chairs and their binoculars and their tickets for a splendid afterlife. J and I weren't worried. We just felt uninformed. We turned to watch the people who were clearly watching something and then we watched that something too—a rocket—though I don't think we ever saw the rocket, just what it left behind, a contrail curving slightly, or maybe just appearing to curve, as it ascended, disappearing behind a high—I want to say *cirrus*—cloud, and then something else must have happened, but I don't know what. Needless to say, it was a disappointment. Later, I learned that Bjarki had seen the very same rocket on the very same day, the SpaceX Something or Other. I admit, I am sometimes shocked when I see sunlight. In the waves, the slick, shining flank rolls again. It is distinctly mammalian. J looks up from his phone and suggests manatee. Manatees have always drifted through me like happiness. I know exactly what to do. That's who you saw that day running barefoot down the beach.

TWO

Canfield

Sixteen months before the rioters stormed the U.S. Capitol, on an autumn afternoon, Bjarki was driving the two of us back to Maine in the rain while at the same time proposing several possible versions of his future self—that person he might become if, or rather *when*, he sold The Wood Mill of Maine, the small lumber business he had purchased seven years prior, in 2012, at the age of twenty-four. On the bench seat of the company pickup, his posture was a casual shrugging slouch. Mostly, he spoke with an emphatic confidence, but he didn't always. There was something tremulous about him, in his breath, in his hands, a timorous bluster that could precipitate action both cautious or headstrong. For instance, when he'd departed his parents' attic in the two golf course town of River Vale, New Jersey, and arrived in dirt road and snowmobile rural Mercer, to take possession of The Wood Mill, he didn't—I'm quoting him now—*know shit about wood.* This, I think, is a source of pride for him. If it had initially seemed to Bjarki that the first and only language spoken at The Wood Mill was a foreign one, it didn't now Now, with relative ease, he could expound on the tree that The Wood Mill's custom boards are sawn from, the eastern white pine, *Pinus strobus*, the tree that had provided frames and floors and furnishings for colonial homes, masts and bowsprits for the British Navy, and the needles for a tea capable of staving off scurvy and flu. Now, in the bark- and snow-covered logs that Bjarki purchases, he sees floors—floors made of boards twenty inches wide and without so much as a pin knot, boards 75 percent wider than the widest available at Lowe's or Home Depot, wider than any pine on the market, wider, in fact, than most of the eastern white pine trees growing in the state of Maine, white whales of the lumber industry, Maine's green gold, American Dream Boards.

He wouldn't sell for less than a million. Then he'd invest the money in a farm-to-table operation, in Iceland, on his family's forty-thousand-acre estate. He'd bring the sheep back to that land and build a dozen log cabins. He'd give chartered helicopter tours. He wanted to fly bush planes. He wanted to live on a boat down in Florida. To motorcycle to Burning Man, the ephemeral community of art and drugs and personal transformation in the Nevada desert. Never would he work for The Man. This he'd known decades earlier, in grade school, when a kindly Waldorf instructor had encouraged him to please continue knitting. "It was like a commune there. You were taught that the world is this good and perfect place, but it isn't. The world is not a Waldorf Safe Zone." In eighth grade, he transferred to public school and though he wasn't unpopular, he was very skinny. Not that he'd been bullied. He just wished he'd helped the kids who were. He wished he'd had more courage. He wanted to be the shepherd. The caretaker, that guy up on the grassy knoll! No, not Joseph. That kid! That kid who walks up the hill and watches over everyone to make sure they're safe! From that super famous American novel?

Dude lives on a hill?

No, he *walks up* the hill.

And he's a shepherd?

Metaphorically.

Jesus, I said.

Bjarki swore.

Several years prior, in June of 2016, Bjarki had delivered a floor to my house on Robinson Street. It was a beautiful pack of pine boards, boards seven, nine, eleven, and thirteen inches wide, boards that to my eyes harkened to a history of house building in Maine, a history I was acquainted with after spending some of my teens, twenties, and thirties helping renovate many of the old stately structures along the Kennebec River near where I lived. In some dark kitchen, under six layers of linoleum and plywood and tile, there were boards an inch thick and twenty-four inches wide. You could see where, two centuries prior, a carpenter had adzed away high spots, or planed the board smooth. You could see the marks of the up and down saw that had cut the board from the log. Sometimes the boards were numbered. Sometimes they turned to dust in your hands.

Bjarki peered at the sky, which was gray, and close, and would be dark in an hour. His hair is short, light brown, and his eyes are set wide in a young face, a round, pale face that seems precariously balanced upon his skinny neck. He sighed. What was now rain had moments before been drizzle. He said the way the air flowed over the pickup, it created a vortex in the truck bed, so that the rain just shot right over as if there was a bubble back there keeping our stuff dry, a couple duffel bags, a pair of boots, the weed-whacker, the DOT-mandated bag of emergency equipment.

He said something about pressure differentials and I said something about Bernoulli and neither one of us really knew what we were talking about. Over the past several years, Bjarki and I had spent a lot of time together in this truck. At times, his particular style of pontification, a sophomoric blend of esoterica and banality, rankled, and at times it was endearing. He could be thoughtful and reflective when discussing himself, but those moments were rare and often masked with bombast and exaggeration, a means of expression that I interpreted as a youthful need to ingratiate himself rather than an attempt to convey an empirical reality. This at first bothered me, for I saw in him those same insecure aspects of my own younger self—a wanting to be accepted and admired—of which I was at times self-conscious. Both Bjarki and I were, of course, white and male and college-educated and living in Maine, the oldest, whitest state in the country, so in terms of acceptance, I'm not talking here about the complicated negotiations of race and class and gender, but rather those quotidian moments in which we find ourselves behaving in a manner contrary to whom we imagine ourselves to be. I wanted Bjarki to stop posturing, to *be himself*—whatever that means. You see, I have always found it difficult to understand that in fact one can *only* be oneself. Who else could you be? Changeability and hypocrisy and performance are parts of who we are. And what is empirical reality, anyway?

The line of red taillight pairs ahead of us stretched and contracted in the rain, shining like something out of the deep sea. For the past three days, in addition to delivering a load of pine floorboards and several jugs of Q8 Log Oil, we'd been visiting Bjarki's mother and sister, who live separately near Newport, Rhode Island. We'd eaten German strawberry cake with mono-grammed silver. Meanwhile, Bjarki's ten-day-old nephew burbled nearby.

"He's not gonna puke on me, is he?" Bjarki asked.

In Bjarki's arms, the baby sneezed two times and Bjarki blessed him twice. Later, we jumped into the family's Mercedes convertible and sped to a bar jammed with tall, slim, smiling white people. In the morning, Bjarki helped power-wash a shed and then he weed-whacked a path to the ocean. There were flowers and bees everywhere.

But Bjarki—he was born in Germany. His mother, Sybille, is German, and his father, Olafur, is Icelandic. After several years working for the "German version of Continental Tire," Olafur became the vice president for Rema Tip Top's North American operations. Rema Tip Top is a rubber products corporation with interests in mining equipment and annual sales near one billion dollars. Bjarki, the second of four children, was two years old when the family moved to New Jersey. One of their first backyards was overgrown with poison ivy. All the kids reacted to it, except Bjarki.

Did I know that Indians are immune to poison ivy?

I did not.

Did I know that a traditional Amish prank involves tossing the shiny leaves into a salad?

I did not.

That goats can eat it without adverse effect?

I had heard that. Later, I read that higher atmospheric levels of carbon dioxide stimulate the plant to produce "significantly more unsaturated uru-shiol," the chemical that causes blistering. As the planet warms, poison ivy will "become more widespread, aggressive, and toxic." Bjarki had recently weed-whacked a patch of *Toxicodendron radicans* near his house in Maine and his arms looked as if he'd stuck them into a furnace. Every day, he was applying a salve of baking soda and vinegar, which kills—he said that, *kills*—the poison ivy. He said he'd never gotten poison ivy before moving to Maine. He said he moved to Maine when he was twenty-two years old. He said he moved to Maine and bought The Wood Mill when he was twenty—twenty-one years old. He said he moved to Maine and bought The Wood Mill when he was twenty-three. He said that his father bought The Wood Mill for him because he'd always dreamt of owning his own business and wanted Bjarki to have that opportunity.

Did I want Bjarki to call Olafur right now?

I did not.

Bjarki called his father.

Olafur said he didn't understand how I could write a whole book about his son. I said I'd call him back. That was on the way *to* Rhode Island.

And also, Bjarki said, he moved to Maine and bought The Wood Mill because he was a big supporter of Maine's gun laws, which he thought emphasized personal freedom and responsibility. He owns thirty-five guns. He owns maybe fifty guns. He owns anywhere from fifteen to twenty guns. He owns assault rifles and shotguns and hunting rifles and pistols and antiques. He buys guns for fun, hunts birds and deer. There's a Sig Sauer P238 handgun on his kitchen counter, a gun in the glove box, long guns above his bed. He'd studied the facts on gun deaths *extensively*. He wanted to talk about Columbine, about doctors overprescribing antidepressants and the media making martyrs out of mass shooters. It was sad. He didn't know what made crazy people tweak. Of course, it's not like *he wanted* to shoot anyone, but sometimes, in the city, he said, "I look around and I think to myself, It could be any one of you motherfuckers."

"That does *what*?"

"That does *something*."

He leaned forward and rolled up the window. The air conditioner was broken and the heater was stuck on and he apologized if I overheated, but he didn't want my tape recorder to lose any of this because of static or interference or whatever from the wind. That would suck, he said, if you lost the one nugget you didn't know you were looking for. Right? Because you have to record everything in case that one snippet turns out to be that one golden nugget?

He paused.

He said he was genuinely curious about how one wrote a book.

In fact, Bjarki was genuinely curious about lots of things, from what my marriage was like to who wrote the *Farmers' Almanac* to how my carpentry business was faring, and often—to my chagrin—I'd respond with a kind of low-grade resentment and animosity. *I* was the one who was supposed to be doing the researching here. Plus, I'm incredibly insecure. See, I *had* written a book before, a collection of essays "about American men," but it never sold, so technically, maybe I had, or maybe I hadn't written a book. Whatever had or hadn't happened, my confidence was low—lower than usual, I mean. I was at that time halfway through my thirty-seventh year and my wife, B, and I were on the verge of separation and we didn't have any kids, and really, if I were to die, who was going to come to my funeral anyway? I mean, I didn't want to die, especially if no one was going to attend my funeral, but recently there *was* this tickling of awareness in me, not only of how few people I actually knew and felt connected to but also of how little I actually knew about The World—whatever that is—as well as myself—ditto. It's unsettling, walking around suspecting you don't have a clue. For instance, I couldn't understand how the floor I'd installed at Robinson Street had turned into such a major disaster, unless, of course, it was a reflection of something majorly disastrous in me.

What I'm trying to say is that I don't know why I didn't dissemble more when Bjarki asked how one writes a book. It's possible that once you've met someone's mother and watched that person hold a ten-day-old child, it's just easier to be honest, which—honesty—frankly, isn't always that easy, especially when it comes to me. Self-honesty feels like the most difficult kind, not because I resist darker truths, but because I tend to speak in hyperbole. I looked out my window, seeing nothing, being entirely in my own thoughts until suddenly, there I was, most of the upper half of me anyway, sort of hovering in or on or behind the glass so that at the same time I saw some of my face lit by the oncoming traffic, I also saw the guardrail and beyond the guardrail where for some reason there were seagulls in the wet humpy grass. It felt like one of those scenes from a book or a movie in which a character sees himself reflected. I have never liked those scenes, probably because I have never understood them.

I said I had no idea how one wrote a book.

"I mean, I find it fascinating that you think I'm *that* interesting, because I don't find myself *that* interesting. And I'm glad that you see a book, because that makes me feel really good, but I feel like I'm always letting you down because I don't have those juicy details I can tell you want. It's like my dad said, 'Maybe you can write ten or fifteen pages about my son, but not a whole book.'"

God, I envied his honesty, the way he wasn't afraid to say he wanted to please me or to say that the thought of a book about him made him feel really good.

But then again, it was heartbreaking—Bjarki's doubts about his own book-worthiness.

Though on the other hand, doubt made sense and was admirable.

Though on the *other* other hand, that stuff his dad had said seemed sort of sad.

I'm a humanist, through and through. See, I said, even if half the time you *are* doing a bunch of nonjuicy stuff, like ruminating or driving or staring at yourself in the mirror or whatever, we're all doing this, this *living*, and it's incredible. Like, for instance, on the left side of my mouth, my second mandibular molar is missing a filling. Doritos compact in that gap. The fibers of broccoli and celery and kale. In lieu of floss, I said, I chew gum aggressively, frequently *and* aggressively. Sometimes, chomping away, I'll develop this dopey swagger, though that day in the truck, even if I was swaggering a little, I still couldn't bring myself to say *everything* I found interesting about Bjarki. Sure, I reiterated all that cool stuff about The Wood Mill and those twenty-inch-wide boards and pine trees and Maine, and I even alluded to craftsmanship and human connection and reality, but what I *didn't* say was that by that point in my research—more than two years in—I'd actually become preoccupied with the things about Bjarki that I found *dis*agreeable— the folksy way he dropped *g*s from participles, for example, and this kind of loud way he breathed, and how he seemed to violently hate Al Gore and his "stupid fucking movie"—*An Inconvenient Truth*—which, he emphasized, he definitely had *not* watched. It was, I admit, a pretty petty catalog. Still, as ugly and contradictory as it all seems now, it's true: though I was at that point rather obsessed with human connection, I was also in thrall to the condescending mockery of gotcha journalism. Bjarki would be the foil by which I exposed the cruel hypocrisies of both privilege and politics. In addition—and this seems even more reprehensible—I thought that I could somehow get Bjarki *to be* less disagreeable. Basically, I thought I could convert him, could make him more like me—ideally, almost exactly like me—someone who admired *An Inconvenient Truth* and didn't mow or weed-whack his lawn and breathed smoothly and evenly. The two of us—identical now—we'd have no trouble forging some kind of deep and meaningful connection and then said con- nection, however forced or coerced, would stand as a kind of undeniable cosmic point for good. It's painful, really, to remember what I was thinking then, even if it all seemed totally reasonable and original, noble even. I was going to make the world a better place.

A police car raced past, its blue siren blaring in the rain.

"*YEEEEEEEEEEOW!*" Bjarki said.

But I do! I blurted out, I *do* want to make the world a better place!

Bjarki—I'm not sure he heard me. He smacked the dash with the flat of his hand. He'd been doing this periodically because the console's gauges and lights functioned only sporadically. At that moment, according to the speedometer, we were stationary, which was of course both true and not.

"Canfield!" Bjarki said. "From that book! *The Catcher in the Rye!*"

"But that's not about a shepherd. That's about a high school kid—"

"—And his name is Canfield."

"*Caulfield.*"

"Holden Caulfield. And he goes up on the hill and watches his girlfriend getting it on with another guy and he gets all emo and depressed."

I thought it was definitely about being a teenager.

"Yeah," Bjarki said. "Like being really confused about life."

Yeah, I said. Yeah. But now *I* was feeling confused—*more confused* than normal, I should say—because I was remembering how, eighteen months prior, we'd actually talked about *The Catcher in the Rye* in this very same truck and Bjarki had said then that it was the last book he'd read and that he hated it because it didn't have *a point*. If you read deep enough into Holden Caulfield's life, you could say it was about anything. You could make all kinds of connections. And didn't, like, crazy people use it to justify all kinds of crazy stuff, like the Bible? Didn't the guy who shot John Lennon think he was the Catcher in the Rye? And maybe Reagan's assassin? And then like two or three other murderers?

I had no idea. It wasn't until later that I went back to my old copy and found that part about the shepherd, which, it turns out, is widely considered to be the book's most famous passage. In it, Holden Caulfield is sort of thinking about what he'd like his purpose in life to be. What he describes is a bunch of kids—thousands of kids   playing in a field of rye right at the edge of some big cliff. He's there too, the only person watching, the shepherd, catching everyone before they go over.

THREE

Shavings (The Little Log Cabin)

You see him through a window. He's on the phone and he's waving you in. He stands up and gives you a thumbs-up. He stands up and gives you a thumbs-down. Nothing for UPS today. On the stoop, pots at eye level overflow with bright flowers. Petunias. A slumping bag of salt. A bottle of Diet Pepsi, chilling. Nearby, a forklift appears poised to skewer the little log cabin and set it like a cupola atop any of the half dozen barns and warehouses spread across the five-acre yard. The yard is slick and rutted with ice. The yard is potholed with brown puddles. Dense forest surrounds you, skinny trees growing thickly, deciduous mostly, not a single pine. There's a tick on your sock. So what if astronomy asserts that the universe has no center; I know better.

A note on the office door announces that this year the price of shavings has risen 40 percent to seven dollars a bag. *This* year is 2020. Everybody wants to know *why*, but do they really *need* to know why?

WIPE YOUR FEET.

Inside, just to the left of the door, Bjarki sits behind the counter in a high-backed rolling chair. He nods, points to the phone, a hands-free headset, the kind that truckers use, like on the open road, like in eighteen-wheelers, tractor trailers, semis, he says, the kind that is noise-canceling and has a special microphone that doesn't pick up any sound from more than like eight inches away. Talk is now possible at eighty miles per hour with the windows down. "Since corona," Bjarki says, this has proven invaluable because Nate's daughters occasionally attend school in the planer building, and at lunchtime, when everyone's in the office, it can sound like a cafeteria in here, like we're employing child labor or something.

"If you want sanitizer, go outside and rub your hands with dirt." These are the inimitable words of Nate Lesperance. Nate manages what happens in the yard, and then some. He's been working at The Wood Mill since he was nineteen, for more than half his life. He's a year older than me. As a person—as a guy—he says, he's not overly complicated. He's not big on gloss. He goes,

"I like it when people don't put on a front, when they just *are*." And what *are* you? I was born in 1982. It's a crapshoot, Nate says, what people like. Some people like knots in their floorboards and some people don't. And some people just want to tell their friends that they spent like twelve grand on a floor. People get all hot 'n' horny over their knotless floor and then they cover it with a rug. What's the word for it when you see something all the time?—not *immune*.

Today, Nate's planing logs for a log home. Today, he's planing siding. He's planing cribbing blocks. A timber frame. Floorboards. All of it produces shavings. The shavings are like time. They get shuttled through ducts and blown out back.

A man, a bag, a shovel. Wind gusts.

Gesundheit!

The woman has red hair. She makes large wooden dice for lawn games.

Standing beside her is a grimacing man, a stonemason, her husband.

Her son, kneeling atop a stool, says, "I didn't know this chair could spin."

The father addresses the son, says, "Let's go get that wood."

The boy spins again and again and then stops abruptly, says, "I've been expecting you."

Yahtzee!

The log cabin's ceiling is pine, planed but untreated, unsealed, unoiled, without gloss, the color of straw and spotted with knots, laid flat over the "collar ties" or the "ceiling joists" or the "girders" or the "timbers" or the "beams" or whatever you prefer to call them so that the small space affects spaciousness despite how much stuff it contains, stuff assembled on shelves and in boxes and on the floor in a manner not incongruous with haphazard: pine board profiles (v-match, t & g, shiplap, S4S, edge and center bead, nickel gap), log profiles, false corners, cedar railing parts (assembled and in pieces), jugs of Waterlox and Q8 Log Oil, nails. Q is *quinolinolate* or oxine copper, apparently. Against the southern wall, below a couple windows and some fading pinups of log homes, a cluttered pine shelf supports me too. I should have said earlier that The Wood Mill of Maine is basically just your local dealer of lumber, though of course it is also something else entirely. *Apophenia* describes the tendency to see meaningful connections between meaningfully disconnected things—life, you might say. On the counter, in a bag of Hershey's Miniatures, only the mr. Goodbars remain. You love mr. Goodbars. ("I love you," I said.

"I know," B said.) There are five pounds of beef jerky in a Ziploc bag. There is a line of radios, a row of cylindrical fuses, seventy-two unsharpened Ticonderoga pencils, an electric pencil sharpener, a stapler, Scotch tape, UPS labels, a carabiner, bullet casings, pizza crusts for Nate's dogs, a book, *The Legend of Silent Horse* by Donald Arthur Clark.

Do you know Donald Arthur Clark?

Don's a former roofer with a master's degree in history. Out in Omaha, he'd slung shingles on an eight-pitch without staging. An eight-pitch, rising eight inches for every twelve that it runs, would give any other Donald the willies. A few years back, when Don retired, he moved to Maine and bought a log cabin from The Wood Mill—or rather, what he bought were *logs* to build a cabin—"D" logs. (B—she's a writer too. She liked to quote a teacher who said that a pile of logs doesn't make a log cabin.) In the meantime, Don has come out of retirement to work three days a week at The Wood Mill, not just for the cash but to help a friend, to help Bjarki.

The Legend of Silent Horse, Bjarki says, is about the Sioux Indians.

Without irony, he says *see-ooks*.

"That's very phonetical of you," says Nate.

You pick up the pine pickup truck parked on the counter. It has pine wheels, a pine steering wheel, pine mirrors, pine bumpers, pine headlights, a pine stick shift. Stacked and stickered on the pine flatbed are miniature pine boards.

"It's, like, holy shit, dude. I don't know if what we did justifies you working *three weeks* to build a truck!"

What did *we* do?

We sold you a bunch of pine.

What'd you do last night, Nate?

"I had a big bowl of Rice Krispies. Then I talked to a couple girls and passed out."

A *menage-a-chat-trois*?

"Nate's last name is Lesperance and he can't even speak French."

Nate shouts *Non!* in French.

All of us shout *Non!* in French.

Bjarki says, "Oui. Baguette. Zee Ei-fell Tow-where."

Nate says, "Guten tag."

Don tells Nate that *guten tag* is German.

Nate tells Don he knows. He says, "I'm multilingual."

The 2020 election was yesterday.

(Or maybe what B said was that adding one more log to the pile won't transform the pile into a cabin? Or, maybe *I mean* that's what B's *teacher* said?) Above Bjarki, clipboards dangle like laundry, or prayer flags, or clipboards, each holding an order, one of which is for nine hundred square feet of flooring, boards seven, nine, and eleven inches wide, to be shipped "right after the Patriots win the Super Bowl." As it turns out, the Patriots do win the Super Bowl this year, in overtime, by six points.

"Nate, I got some bad news."

"What you got?"

"If the phone rings, pardon me, I got to grab it."

The phone rings.

"Good afternoon, The Wood Mill." It's a practiced salutation that inflects and accelerates, the *good* drawn out, the *the* almost dropped. Both Nate and Bjarki answer the phone similarly.

"Yeah, just talk slowly maybe. That way it won't get chopped up too bad." It's a poor connection.

Nate says, "Shavings from a board will be pretty fluffy and curly, but more on the small side. Shavings from log siding will be really long, fat and curly. When we do logs, it's a bit of everything, from kinda chunky to kinda sawdusty to kinda curly. We don't separate types of shavings."

My therapist says that you are made up of parts and that these parts are literally a bunch of different *you*s inside you, trying to help you, sometimes in ways that aren't entirely helpful. She doesn't say *where* these parts are inside you. Nor does she define *you*. Can you define *you*? You pop the chocolate into your mouth, completely unaware of it becoming you, Mr. Goodbar, you who stand upon a pine board twenty inches wide. Like a welcome mat directly inside the door, the board is scuffed from foot traffic. This is how The World walks in here.

"The doctor said, 'Looks like you got a clump of ear wax in there,' and he prodded around and the pain was intolerable and he goes, 'Oh, that's not wax. That's a scab.' That was three weeks ago. I soaked it in my Whirlpool with Epsom salt. I get my ear in front of the jet and cup my fingers to get some water moving without the pressure and after, I told Ma, 'The fuckin' ear feels better.'"

"What causes ear infections?"

Myke Bartholf, the man who sold Bjarki the two companies that would become The Wood Mill of Maine, says that removing the scab caused the infection.

"But what caused the scab?"

Sand and pea-sized gravel from unwiped feet crunch underfoot. There's a water jug on the floor, shavings on the floor, blood on the floor. Tattooed on Nate's left bicep are his initials, N. H. L., the letters formed by birds, by slim black storks.

"Why storks?"

"Well, why not?"

When Nate says *well* it sometimes sounds like *wool*. *Wool*, that wide pine board on the floor that you're calling a twenty-incher is technically a nineteen-and-a-half-incher. In fact, there are *two* twenty-inchers in the floor. They blend in until they don't.

"You should write about the blind carpenter," Bjarki says.

"Want to hear a dad joke?" Nate says.

"Good morning, The Wood Mill."

The man tells Nate he has twelve bags of shavings in his truck, for his pigs. One thousand square feet of pine pushed through the planer will produce enough shavings to fill just more than a dozen bags.

"Sixty bucks," says Nate.

It's not 2020 yet.

"Shavings?"

"Yes." The woman's hands are in the front pocket of her sweatshirt.

"They're seven dollars a bag."

The woman removes a checkbook from her pocket. She wears gold rings on pink fingers.

Bjarki says, "L still around?"

The woman says, "He's in the truck."

In the driver's seat of the truck parked outside is a man with a bushy—I'll call it a Whitmanesque—beard.

The woman leaves and the truck drives away.

Bjarki remembers L aloud, his size, his age. "He used to send guys for shavings who reeked of the cow manure."

Nate says, "This one old guy, he'd have us fill out checks for him, sign his name and everything. He was just totally illiterate. It's like, old people who grew up on farms—"

Oxen halted in the shade of pines, what is it in your eyes?

It seems to me more than I have read in all my life.

"—It's like, 'What do I need to learn to read for?'"

TRESPASSING

VIOLATORS

WILL BE SHOT

Below the security camera, on Bjarki's desk, there's a pistol-grip pump-action shotgun, barrel up. An NRA ball cap dangles. There are no shopping carts here, no aisles, no customer service reps in matching aprons, no uniform corporate scent, no preapproved soundtrack, no cash register, no lines, two vacuums, a twelve-pack of empty Budweiser bottles. The trash needs to go out. I smell beef jerky. For lunch, Bjarki orders a salad for *Bobby*.

"*B* as in *boy*, *J* as in *jet*, A-R-K-I."

On the phone, Bjarki says, "Yeah, the writer."

Tomorrow's Election Day 2020. I've been doing some carpentry work at a camp twenty minutes south of here, in Rome, near where the legendary North Pond Hermit lived in a tarp encampment for twenty-six years.

The blood on the floor is not blood, it's ketchup. Or maybe it's marinara.

"*Generic!*" Nate says. A wide pine board, to him, just looks *generic*. According to the Northeastern Lumber Manufacturers Association (NeLMA), a select board (the highest quality NeLMA board) must have fewer than one half-inch knot per linear foot. Flaws—scars really—like splits, pitch, checks, shake, and stain are permitted, though in a limited quantity. The Wood Mill of Maine scorns NeLMA standards. Bjarki's select boards—the ones I'm here to tell you about—they depend on a premise of blemishlessness. They are knotless and flawless, marked only by graceful ribbons of grain. On the office's windowless wall, several of these boards hang vertically, shining dully like tapestry.

Shavings (The Magazine-Style Essay)
(January 31, 2017)

FIVE

Rangoon

In retrospect, the dinner that seemed to hasten our separation and almost brought the whole thing to a halt took place in a Thai restaurant very early in the process of researching what I was at that time calling a magazine-style essay. It was the middle of April 2017, about two and a half years before Bjarki and I drove to Rhode Island, or about a month after we went ice fishing, which was about three months after our initial interview in The Wood Mill of Maine's office, or about two years after B and I purchased the house on Robinson Street, the house outside of which I first met Bjarki sixteen months later. I mean, I met Bjarki for the first time sixteen months after B and I purchased the house. Before that, we'd been living in a cramped apartment in an expansive Wyoming valley. The moon out there was the biggest I've ever seen. Our neighbor married us. Then we moved to Maine.

I was born in Boston, but I grew up in Woolwich, a rural community across the Kennebec River from Robinson Street, which is in Bath. Not directly across, but about six or seven miles upriver—that's where I grew up. In Maine, I mean. The chronology and geography may be confusing because it's all in my mind at once now and I want to get it exactly right, at least to a degree. There is also everything that came after that dinner, including the moment three years later, when, in the same restaurant, in the same booth, I fell in love with Bjarki. I'm serious. That whole place was made of brick.

It was called Thai Smile and it was located in Farmington, about fifteen miles west of Mercer and The Wood Mill. Mercer, with fewer than seven hundred residents, is bordered to the north by the Sandy River, a tributary of the Kennebec that tumbles out of Moosehead Lake and then, after flowing 150 miles south, passes my house—a half-mile wide and tidal, reversing the direction of its flow every six hours, saltier at high tide, brackish always. I can see it while I'm writing, between trees and the roofs of houses: a blue stripe or a white stripe or a black stripe or a brown stripe or a green stripe or a gray stripe or a ribbon or a band or a swath or some other variation or combination or manifestation depending on the season and the time of day. And me too, of course. To say a river is just one thing is something I am trying not to say. I read poetry only rarely. Below Robinson Street, the Kennebec elbows sharply east at Winnegance, across from the remains of the tidal sawmills, and then it passes the octagonal lighthouse at Doubling Point and bends south again toward the cold waters of the Gulf of Maine. There, in the year 1607, where the Kennebec enters the sea, at the failed Popham colony, *Virginia*, the first ship built in the New World—*New World*: a silly, if apt, designation—and subsequently sailed to Europe was constructed, thus initiating the area's long history of shipbuilding renown. Five thousand ships would eventually be launched from Bath. By 1850, it was the fifth largest port in America— whatever that means—and many of its homes were built during that boom time. The ship captains' ornate and sometimes ostentatious mansions with their widow's walks and Grecian columns mostly populate the northern side of town while the houses around Robinson Street are more modest, well proportioned, clapboarded, with sidelit entries and slim chimneys. A slim chimney dates an old house's construction to after the first quarter of the nineteenth century. Before that, chimneys were wider, supporting multiple fireplaces—fireplaces that sent 80 percent of a fire's warmth straight up rather than out into a room. Early homes may have burned forty cords of wood each year. Stacked, forty cords makes a pile four feet tall and four feet wide and three hundred twenty feet long. As early as 1638, there were reports of firewood shortages around Boston. Trees in colonial America were cut for buildings, fences, and barrel staves, to clear agricultural land, to make iron and charcoal and bricks. Tannins cured animal hides. Potash—potassium nitrate—was needed to make soap and glass. Boat builders coveted white oak for its strength and resistance to rot. Masts were made of the supremely straight, lightweight, and flexible white pine.

In addition, New Englanders cleared forests with missionary zeal, believing the shade sheltered Satan and his minions—namely, wolves, witches, and Indians. By 1850, half of the northeast's forest cover had been felled. In his 1799 *Travels through the States of North America*, the Irishman Isaac Weld observed that Americans

have an unconquerable aversion to trees; and whenever a settlement is
made, they cut away all before them without mercy; not one is spared;
... they are looked upon as a nuisance, and the man that can cut down
the largest number, and have the fields about his house most clear of
them, is looked upon as the most industrious citizen, and the one that
is making the greatest improvements in the country.

The house on Robinson Street, built in 1855 by John C. Harris, once had
two slim chimneys, though only one remains today. John and Cyrus are my
middle names. Robinson Street was once Harrison Street. Before that, I don't
know. Bjarki arrived on a sweltering morning in June. My floor, strapped
to the back of his pickup, was wrapped completely in plastic to prevent the
infiltration of humidity. Wood expands and contracts as its moisture content
changes. It was imperative, Bjarki said, that I lay the floor as soon as possible,
get it nailed down and sealed.

These boards are literally sponges, he said. Did I understand that?

Only in retrospect is it clear how very little I have understood. I mean, B
and I hadn't explicitly intended to depart Wyoming and return to the turf of
my childhood. She'd gotten a job nearby and the house on Robinson Street—
foreclosed on and vacant for five years—was exactly what we were looking
for, which was old and a total gut. We weren't exactly thriving financially, so
though we did technically buy the house, it was my dad who loaned us the
money, stipulating such generous terms that it might as well have been a gift.
I'm not sure how specific I want to be about all of this, but for me, our future
house—Robinson Street lovingly renovated—promised a kind of salvation.
The whole place pitched east, toward the river, about an inch for every six feet.
I mean, I wouldn't say our relationship was crumbling like the house's lone
skinny chimney, but in the roof there *were* the requisite leaks. There was the not
insignificant tributary of the Kennebec flowing off the ledge in the basement
and out a rough hole in the stone foundation. There were broken windows
and busted drainpipes and there was crumbling plaster and wiring twisted in
confusing snarls, nibbled through by squirrels, some of which I found mum-
mified in the walls and floors. In fact, there were so many gray squirrels living
inside that the neighbors referred to our house as the Squirrel House.

Squirrels have always been something of a spirit animal for B—which, *spirit animal*, neither of us knew to be a potentially problematic term—so when I trapped and then transported them across the Kennebec, I liked to think that they saw me as a great liberator, but who knows. I have always resided in fantasy and dreams. B and I were at this point living with our anthropophobic cat in the basement of my childhood home, in Woolwich, literally under my parents' feet. We would go on walks in the evening, a jar of bourbon between us. There was Orion. There was the Big Dipper and the North Star and Ursa Minor, which, oddly, was either a little bear or a little ladle. (Bjarki, in Icelandic, means *little bear*. (I hadn't yet met Bjarki.)) Do you hear the ice in the river? What is the difference between the shattering sounds of separation and the shattering sounds of collision? There are lightning bugs out here in the summer. Or fireflies. I mean, everything in a dream is symbolic. I don't want to overanalyze it. We rarely had a flashlight, preferring the gradual adjustment of our eyes to the night. I remember once the silence and the moon in the snow and B crying because she didn't know how much longer she could do *this* and me telling her that it would only be another month before we moved out of the basement and into the attic at Robinson Street and that then we'd be fine again, and better than before. I was serious. As a proposition, it seemed reasonable. I'd rig up a makeshift sink and stove. We'd shower at the Y, plant a garden, write in our time's margins. This is what I mean by dreams. It sounded so romantic I almost convinced myself it was possible, and maybe it was, though we didn't move in for another year and a half.

I wasn't yet five years old when my family arrived in Woolwich. This may or may not make me a Masshole, one of those tourists who drive like jerks, occupy the biggest coastal houses, and demand fancy coffee. Real Mainers— whomever they are—are quite territorial, it seems, and proud. Anyway, though I grew into a tall, popular—if not totally cool—kid, at times I felt a great gulf between myself and my peers, a separateness that felt essential and therefore devastating. My father—not a Real Mainer—was a doctor and I was insecure about his figurative white collar, even though he never wore shirts with literal white collars. He wore amazing necklaces. For instance, I had never shot a gun or driven a snowmobile or gone ice fishing—all of which my buddies talked about with sweaty reverence and joy. I'm serious. They wanted to shotgun beers. Have you ever sprayed WD-40 over a lit match? That is a revelatory experience. Grade school and high school are getting all mixed up for me here. I remember distinctly kids being removed from class because of the way they smelled, the way they banged staples into their foreheads, the way they slept the whole day or shouted or cried, it seemed, for no reason. I did not understand why some teachers favored me while subjecting others to discipline and ridicule. Everyone was supposed to be equal. No one was inherently bad. No one was lesser than, etc., etc.

Did I like eel?

Bjarki was pretty sure there was eel in the Dragon Roll.

I loved eel, which meant Bjarki and I loved the same thing, which at the time didn't seem important. He'd once caught an eel in the Sandy River behind his house, hooked the writhing four-footer with a scrap of chicken, and cut off its head with a machete. In a bucket, for like two hours, the decapitated eel swam figure eights backward.

"Eels," he said, "don't even need a head to live."

His enthusiasm that night was so sincere I could hardly stand it. See, even though I love it when anyone gets excited, sometimes I don't love it. It's pretty arbitrary, I admit, and I'm not proud of it—how judgmental and condescending and superior I can be, even though I know it is sometimes important to condemn that which conflicts with what is Good and Proper in The World. It's just, what is Good and Proper? And when is it good and proper to defend the Good and Proper?

The chef's name, Bjarki said, was *Chalee*. Whereas I believed in speed limits, Bjarki did not. He was fifteen years old when he took the stick of a friend's twin-wing single-prop stunt plane—a Pitts Special—and invited it to barrel-roll. Below him lay the dramatic landscape of northern Iceland, where, during the summers of his teenage years, he taught sailing amid occasional icebergs. "I've flown a lot of small planes," he said. "Not legally, but—" We watched a video.

The plane rolled.

Bjarki, inverted, yowled gloriously.

"7Gs," he said. "I loved it."

Or maybe I was just annoyed because it seemed like Bjarki was auditioning to be a really exciting character in a magazine-style essay, or because when he asked if *I'd* done all kinds of "wild stuff" growing up, I hadn't known what to say—was catching frogs *wild*?—and as a result, not only did I somehow feel inferior or uncool but I also sensed that Bjarki thought less of me, which of course was just my own projection.

But what I'm trying to say here is that, at least on some level, in doing carpentry I have for a long time considered myself an interloper in a world of men who earn their living with their hands—a misconception several times over, I know. For one thing, carpentry is just as much brains as hands. For another, the world of men is a yellow myth. To say the headless backward swimming eel was alive was probably a mistake. Still, sometimes I wonder if guilt—about privilege, about class—turned me to more manual work, and if so, did that disingenuousness—if that's what it was—somehow undermine the skills I had acquired or make me a bad person? (Of course not.) But I guess what I'm really asking, more generally, is how much self-interest is okay, like Right and Proper, and when do my desires and motivations undermine a project. I mean, I say that I want to make the world a better place, but if I really do want that, aren't there more appropriate subjects to be writing about? Or maybe I am writing about a couple of privileged bros in order to interrogate that privilege? Or maybe I'm *not* trying to expose and indict privilege at all but attempting personal absolution in order to more guilt-lessly enjoy the fruits of *my privilege*, and if that's the case, then wouldn't that delegitimize what I'm writing here? And isn't the desire to make the world a better place really just the Most Privileged Desire, a divine impulse born from exploitation and gluttony? After all, infantilism is a kind of luxury. In four billion years, when the sun swallows the Earth, do not let me be alone.

After B and I moved into Robinson Street, I went back to work for the guys I'd learned carpentry from in high school and college, a well-respected crew of clean-shaven Christians—E and G and B (not *B*)—who, on Mondays, thanked the Lord and asked Him to bless our hands. That was cool, that your hands could possess a skill not your own. My bosses cut laser-straight lines without fretting. They made seams disappear. I loved their language, their accents, the way they called me *Matty*. A board that was too big was *proud*, or *strong*, while a board that was too small was *shy*, but not weak. A cut with the grain was a *rip*, an angle across the grain was a *miter*, and an angled rip was a *bevel. Wane. Cup. Crown. King jack, stringer, rafter, stud.*

The old houses we worked in had been built without plywood, without the rot-resistant, water-repellant, pre-painted, taped, caulked, sprayed, and sealed building systems sold to the modern homebuilder. America's earliest houses were constructed with whatever was readily available, which was often enough pine. It was lightweight, plentiful, and easy to work with. Exterior trim was milled from pine. Clapboards were pine. Shingles were pine. Wainscoting and cupboards and doors were pine. Floors were pine.

Today, *Pinus strobus*, or eastern white pine, isn't often associated with flooring. White pine is a fast-growing tree, a softwood lacking density and, as lumber, stability. In a floor, the boards gap. Underfoot and under furniture, they dent. They scratch, scuff, and stain. Often, with disdain, carpenters will say that pine is *camp wood*, meaning simply that it is cheap or common, more appropriate for the seasonal cabins Mainers call *camps* rather than, say, some Masshole's *cottage*. There is, of course, nothing inherently wrong with that. And neither is a cottage inherently superior to a camp. Or vice versa. I only mean to suggest that there exists an assumed hierarchy of contemporary flooring materials and pine falls somewhere near the basement, below your oak and your maple, your birch, your bamboo, and your fir.

The widest pine board I found in my house was sixteen inches wide and I saved it. I saved all the widest boards from the walls and subfloor, materials that ye olde carpenter never intended to be seen but that are now considered objects of aesthetic and antiquarian reverie. I made sawhorses out of this scavenged stuff, cutting tenons with a pull saw and a chisel, easing the sharp corners with a plane. I enjoyed making them. Also, I admit, my adoring construction was an attempt to more authentically render that handmade, reclaimed aesthetic that is now so ubiquitous it is displayed on the walls of McDonald's, printed on Pergo floors as *antique barnwood*, satirized on Craigslist. (Of course, there is nothing inherently wrong with barnwood that has never been a part of a barn.) As Bjarki and I carried my first floor inside and stacked it upon those horses, as we exchanged biographical notes and he expounded on the nature of pine, I was swiftly coming to see him as a kind of antidote to this culture of mass-produced imitation. He was an authentic craftsman, in touch with something real. I wanted to touch something real. Who didn't? I could see it so clearly in my mind—the magazine-style essay— and as I gazed upon it, I became more and more enthusiastic, so much so I can hardly stand it now. Bjarki would become my very own flooring master, my coniferous sensei, my Obi-Wan of Knotlessness, imparting to me all of his accumulated woody wisdom—unfortunate phrase—which would then lead me to some kind of ecstatic realization, of what, I didn't know, though I was sure it would forever change me for the better.

His phone rang.

"Hey, let me call you later. All right. Bye."

It was his father.

He said, "I don't want to be the asshole on the phone in a restaurant."

I said I wouldn't have called him an asshole.

"Yeah," he said, "but my dad would."

Right, in retrospect, maybe I should have followed up on that comment about his dad and phones and assholes, but at that point I couldn't imagine any dads in my magazine-style essay. Instead, I asked Bjarki about sailing. I knew he had learned to sail at the age of six and that he'd sailed competitively at Roger Williams University and I envisioned writing a couple of sentences relating the mystical aspects of woodworking to the mystical aspects of sailing.

"Well," Bjarki said, "you've got to read the currents, read the wind, read everything."

All judgment, I did not at the time think, is misjudgment and condescending. Nor did I think then that platitudes are not always platitudinal. Of course you could also truthfully say that there are no aspects that are not mystical. I am of the tribe who believe that being able to see everything clearly, or read it, or whatever you do with it—whatever it is—that will enlighten us, make us better, or maybe Good, and even though the Mystical Nature of Everything really was what I wanted Bjarki to talk about, had always wanted him to talk about, wanted everyone to talk about, as wildly inappropriate as that might be, I'm sure the reason I didn't pursue the matter was because since our first meeting on Robinson Street I had come to believe that Bjarki couldn't enlighten me. Or maybe—and this seems even more deplorable—I didn't *want* him to, as if it matters *who* enlightens us. It was pretty confusing. I had been looking up and now I was looking down. I don't even believe superiority *is* an empirical possibility and yet there I was feeling superior. And *enjoying* it. And at the same time I was also disliking myself intensely. I mean, I'm trying to change. I'm trying to be more open and equanimous and nonjudgmental while at the same time trying not to think that this will make me a *better* person, as in *better* than my old self, or *better* than you. I mean, I believe all that equanimity stuff *will* make me a better person, just not a *better* person. My thinking on the matter is what in high school we would have called a *cluster*. (In high school, some kids were called *scummy* or *scurvy* or *skanky* or *skuzzy*.) B always said that people can't change, and while I think she's right, I think she's wrong too. I mean, people are always changing, and not just in terms of what they're feeling and their actual position in space and their specific atomic makeup and all that. There's another kind of change that I believe in too. Or maybe B meant change is impossible on a more soul-type level, like, you are who you are, with which I also agree. I can see how that's a contradiction, but it's also not a contradiction. Or maybe what B was really suggesting had to do with agency, like that change happens *to you* and that *you* can't change who you are, with which I also agree. Or maybe she just meant that she didn't think *I* could change. I don't know. One of the un-changing constants in all of us that I do believe in is the no-one-is-better-than-anyone-else quality of being—that great American platitude. I'm serious. No one is better than anyone else. I guess what I'm trying to say is that it's pretty confusing—feeling this superiority—and uncomfortable, and sometimes in my confusion I resent you, like, Stop making *me* feel superior. Just be better! It's very immature, I know. Or maybe it's totally natural and normal.

I mean, so much depends upon a mattress. At dinner that night, my blood sugar was—I'm sure—plunging and spiking erratically, and so when Bjarki said something about a college drinking game called a Boat Race, I kind of snorted, and then was immediately consumed by self-loathing and dismay and in an attempt, perhaps, to absolve myself, I knew that I must try—earnestly try—to achieve the real human connection I was allegedly so desperate to make and so, haltingly and sincerely, I confessed that college, for me, had really been a staggering introduction to the superlative fruits of the supposed American Dream. Dollar bills blew across that campus like snow in a blizzard. I was cold with the feeling of less. Actually, that isn't totally honest. There was always Ben and Jerry's ice cream in the cafeteria. See, even as I was trying to connect with Bjarki—or *thought* I was trying to connect with Bjarki—I was also hoping to get him to say something about *his* privilege. I mean, over and over, every time I tried to get Bjarki to say what I wanted him to say, to manipulate him, I mean, to change him into a Bjarki best suited for my magazine-style essay, he stubbornly refused. In fact, he lit right up when I mentioned the small private college I'd attended in Vermont. There'd been protests there recently, around the planned speech of Dr. Charles Murray, coauthor of *The Bell Curve*, a book that may argue that some people are innately *better* than others. The protesters, Bjarki said, hate the constitution. *Hate*—that's the word he used.

We had by this point strayed so far from my fantasy of Bjarki the *Pinus strobus* Jedi that I had reverted to that compulsive-eating thing where you just shovel and chew, shovel and chew, tasting nothing. You can hear my steady masticating on the recording and then my sudden shock about finding cream cheese in what I've just eaten and then Bjarki's laughing because That's what crab rangoon is, he says, crab and cream cheese, as if this is something everyone knows, which I didn't at that time know, and immediately I found myself feeling more than slightly insecure about my status as a Rangoon Ignoramus and therefore defensive and also angry. In fact, I remember thinking that cream cheese and crab should never be married, as if foods and flavors haven't always been mating and migrating, as if there exists some kind of unchanging cultural caloric purity, like people *shouldn't* enjoy crab and cream cheese together even if they do in fact enjoy crab and cream cheese together. I don't even know what makes cheese, cheese. Rangoon though, it turns out, is actually the former capital city of Burma, which became Myanmar in 1989, at the same time that Rangoon became Yangon. The new capital of Myanmar is Naypyitaw, which is north of Yangon. There is no Rangoon anymore, only crab rangoon, which, I read later, came about in San Francisco along with the rise of tiki culture—pineapples, thatched roofs, coconut bras—as WWII soldiers returned home from Hawaii and Southeast Asia. (Thailand and Myanmar are neighbors, geographically.) (The most ancient traces of

Pinus strobus pollen were discovered in a Shenandoah Valley lakebed and were determined to be sixteen thousand years old.) (*Pinus strobus* first arrived in Maine about twelve thousand years ago, behind the southern edge of the receding glaciers.) In Wyoming, I got on my knees.

B was in the blue chair, holding a glass of red wine. The floor was carpeted. I guess she was flabbergasted.

She said, "Are you fucking serious?"

I hadn't even considered. I mean, I guess I thought I was.

Everything okay? The waiter was standing beside our table. Everything okay?

Excellent, Bjarki said.

Everything, I said.

Did I want to run back to Bjarki's place and get toasted?

I didn't.

Did I still party?

I made an ambiguous sound.

"From time to time?"

I was by then so thoroughly worn down that I was like, Sure, *fine*, I party from time to time—*from time to time!* It's all on tape. Like a goddamn sage I said it. I said, "The secret is water." It's not beer before liquor or whatever. It's just water. Water is not a symbol here or anything, I said. It's just what I said, I said. Men, on average, need to ingest about three liters a day. Human bones are composed of 31 percent water. Bjarki's boards have a moisture content of about 7 percent. A tree's ability to bring water from its roots to the tips of its branches by capillary action may limit how tall it can grow. I was looking intensely at Bjarki—willing him to comprehend me—and he, responding in the most friendly check-out-this-cool-new-fact way, told me that beer actually *doesn't* hydrate you at all. Beer, he said, *dehydrates* you.

And instead of sharing in Bjarki's wonder regarding the dehydrating properties of booze, I found myself feeling even more superior, and then instantly I also felt unsettled by that feeling and, stubbornly mushing on, I said, Fun fact: did you know that on March 16, 1621, Samoset, an Abenaki man, greeted the Pilgrims in spoken English and then requested beer, but because the Pilgrims had no beer, they gave him distilled brandy, which they called "strong water"?

It's true, I can be melodramatic. When friends asked how it felt to have finally moved into Robinson Street, I told them it was like living inside the book that I had written, even though I'd never actually written a *real* book— unless you counted that unpublished collection of essays, which apparently I didn't. I was thinking about the gaps between the ideal and the real, between promise and compromise, success and failure, but the way I said it, I think my friends liked my analogy or metaphor or whatever it was because it sounded like a happy thing. People always want things to be one way or the other. You are either better or you aren't. You either love her or you don't. The house is either done or it isn't. I don't know why we see things so dualistically. I mean, I can see why. Still, I can also see how much that simplified vision misses—how much we all always necessarily miss. As I walked through the house—giving the tour—I always felt surrounded by mirrors. It was the most hyperbolized version of that scene in books and movies that I can't stand, myself reflected everywhere, in the missing thresholds and drawer fronts and trim, the unhung doors, The Wood Mill of Maine floor I'd somehow ruined. I was giving tours of myself. Is that not the most solipsistic thing you've ever heard? I mean, I know *why* I thought fixing a house could fix a relationship. An Aquarian can do anything. Though at the same time, there is nothing he can do. This was probably why I liked sitting on the flimsy porch that jutted off the kitchen. It felt separate from the house somehow, outside of whatever I had or hadn't fixed or finished, flush still with possibility. B and I liked to watch the moon rise over the river out there.

"The moon seems to change," one of us would say.

"But the moon does not change," the other would say.

Those were lines from a picture book.

I looked menacingly over the small candle flame toward Bjarki and I didn't even thank him for the invitation to run back to his place and get toasted—whatever *toasted* was. Instead, I said I wanted to run back to Rangoon Street and enjoy a couple of rangoons on the porch and just totally obliterate Rangoon. Then I cringed, both at what I had said and also what I had not said. It was quite possible that parts of me were envious of Bjarki's ease with his privilege, his ease with his father giving him The Wood Mill and his ease with himself, though at the same time it was also possible that the ease I saw as he toured me through his life was actually a well-disguised discomfort. Who knows what Bjarki was thinking and feeling in that moment. Did he even know? Does anyone ever know? I mean, we were just two white dudes in a Thai restaurant in central Maine, a whole bunch of water in very specific form, our invisible respiration mingling, carrying all the bits of DNA and deep fry and feeling and fact that exhales contain, passing back and forth between us, in and out of us, becoming more of us and less of us, for better or for worse or for neither or for both.

SIX

Shavings (Split (Afterward))

The first thing Hitler did was disarm the Jews. Mao and Mussolini too. If you had given a starving Chinese man a rifle, oh my goodness, can you imagine? One of my favorite memes is this Vietnamese guy with a hat and an AK-47. It says, "Laughs in Viet Cong," meaning: you can have all the technology you want, fancy laser beams and drones, but the people in sandals with zero military experience will win.

"So I don't trust the government. That's not a conspiracy theory. All the government does is fuck you."

"People throw the word *Nazi* around. Whenever they disagree with you, they call you a Nazi. Nazis were actually Socialists. They weren't far right. They were far *left*."

"Open your eyes."

Beside me is a can of Outlast Q8 Log Oil, a wood preservative specifically designed to "control decay causing organisms."

I'm feeling a little discomfited in the office, and I think Bjarki can tell. It's an olive branch, of a kind, when he shows me the photos of a woman he recently met on Tinder.

"K," he says, "she's the Polish Tinderella. Nate thinks we look alike."

I flick through Bjarki's phone. There's K in the mountains, in Iceland, on European streets, and then—there's Bjarki! Or, rather, there's K looking like Bjarki, which is weird because K doesn't look like a man and Bjarki doesn't look like a woman.

"She's got way better teeth than me."

As a point of fact, Bjarki's teeth are fine.

He says, "We already talked about how my grandfather invaded her country."

"The Viking?" I'm confusing grandfathers.

"The German," Bjarki says.

"The Nazi," Nate says.

"So, ah, K goes, 'What do you think of Jewish people?'"

Nate says, "Crap."

"I think she wanted to make sure I'm not a Nazi."

Nate sighs loudly. He says, "I don't like dating. It's horrible."

Bjarki explains that his mother's father was drafted into the German army and then shot down over France. He says the leg he broke in the crash eventually had to be rebroken.

Incidentally, a few days later, in Rhode Island, over German strawberry cake at Bjarki's mother's house, Sybille's father will come up in conversation. Sybille is talking about raising her children. She says, "We have the saying, 'You grow with your tasks,' but today, I'm thinking, How did I do that? I got all four kids dressed and I still baked muffins to take to the pond. And you were always dressed nicely with shirts and collars." She holds her fork to her mouth. "Then there was *my mom*, who ironed *underwear*, and my father, who insisted to have his *socks* ironed." Her father was born in 1919 and drafted into the "old Prussian army." He became a dentist after the war. Her grandfather served on a submarine in World War I.

Bjarki says, "Was it your grandfather or your father who's leg was broken?"

On the kitchen counter is a fake beach sign:

TO SHOWER - $1

TO WATCH - $2

"One of them had a broken leg that didn't heal right and they had to rebreak it."

"I do not know about that. My father, he was a navigator on a plane. He was reading a map and got shot down."

"And he broke his leg! He was in a POW camp with a broken leg."

Sybille says he was shot in the lung.

Bjarki says he can't imagine how they rebroke that bone in, like, the *forties*.

I suggest baseball bat.

Bjarki suggests vise.

Nate suggests wood splitter.

We are talking about a leg that may actually never have been broken, let alone *rebroken*, but we don't know that. We are having a good time. We are pals.

"They bring in this big German guy—"

"Whose name is definitely Hans, like the Russian in *Rocky*."

"*If he dies, he dies.*"

Nate says *Rocky* is a great movie. He says, "It's a bad movie, but it's also a great movie."

Bjarki says, "Who was the karate guy who got chubby?"

"Chuck Norris?"

"Maybe he's Mexican?" Bjarki says.

"Steven Seagal!"

"He was a *real* badass."

"Whatever the hand-to-hand combat is, he was one of the best. He just sucked at acting."

"Was he American? Or was he Mexican?"

Nate says Seagal was definitely not Mexican. On his phone, he's looking up whatever the hand-to-hand combat is.

In the meantime, Bjarki shows me a Volvo commercial featuring another action movie star, Jean-Claude Van Damme—eyes closed, arms folded—standing on two tractor trailers, one foot on the side mirror of each truck.

Nate says he was born in Michigan.

"Van Damme?"

"Seagal."

He opens his eyes. The golden sun is either rising or setting. There is beautiful singing. The trucks are gold and they are backing up.

"Dude," Bjarki says. "You know how hard it is to back up a trailer? They're reversing two! This is literally the best commercial I've ever seen! This is one hundred percent real!"

The trucks begin to separate, the gap between them widening.

"It's real! It's real!"

"Aikido!"

"*Ha*kido or *a*ikido?"

"*A*. He's a seventh-something-degree black belt in *a*ikido."

"Isn't this unreal?"

My mind fails to behave as instructed. The trucks, still backing up, must be five or six feet apart now and Van Damme is straddling the space between them, his legs spread and parallel to the ground. This, he says, is *the most epic of splits.*

(Bjarki and I are sitting at the bar in his kitchen, eating reheated dinners from a Hannaford grocery. Eighteen hundred dollars lies in a stack beside an odd spice jar–looking thing: an artificial deer call. The label says, SPEAK THE LANGUAGE.

I say, "Is this fish or pork?"

Cat Stevens jumps onto the bar and Bjarki sets him on the floor. Mr. Crowley's hiding.

"So what'd you do down there," he asks, meaning Florida.

"I got clipped by a car."

"Did you get hit head-on?"

Over the winter, Bjarki and the woman he'd been dating, A, split up, though whether they were ever really together is not beyond dispute. Nothing happened with K. I've never met A. She's the one who adopted these two kittens that are quickly becoming cats.

Phwap, phwap: that's the cat door.

Bjarki offers to send a message to a friend who is recently single.

He says, "hippie" and "babe," and I say, "Jesus" and "sure."

Cat Stevens, on the counter, chews a roll of paper towels.

"They're real snugglers at night. I couldn't split with them. I love 'em." The tabby brothers have pink noses, but Bjarki is fascinated by their differences. Mr. Crowley's fur is grayer and coarser and Cat Stevens has what I think of as thumbs, a trait that Bjarki says there's a word for and that I believe there's a word for, though neither of us know the word. Bjarki shakes some Meowijuana onto a scratching post. Mr. Crowley emerges and attacks the post. Cat Stevens flops with a stuffed fish. The word is *polydactyl.*

On his phone, Bjarki plays the Ozzy Osbourne song, "Mr. Crowley," and we kind of sing along. Almost anyone can sound okay if they sing softly enough.

"*Your lifestyle to me seems so*—what is it?"

"Fantastic?"

It's *tragic.*

"It's just a kick-ass, badass song. And it made me think of cats, because what the fuck are cats thinking half the time?"

We listen again, this time on the stereo.

Bjarki says, "Aleister Crowley was a devil worshipper, supposedly."

I say, "The fact that Ozzy sings the word *afterbirth* is so awesome."

"Every line in this song is symbolizing something, but if you're looking for how it relates to me, it's not to be found."

"It's about *me*," I say.

A week or so before I left for Florida—on the eve of the election—Bjarki and I had been talking about getting away from it all, a topic that came up frequently and that I thought had the potential to humanize Bjarki, in The Book, I mean, because of course Bjarki already existed as a human. To that end, I adopted a hands-off policy as our conversations ranged from road trips to the North Pond Hermit to Henry David Thoreau to Burning Man to Chris McCandless, the twenty-four-year-old who died in the Alaskan wilderness. *Into the Wild* was written about him, a movie made.

"McCandless—he did something. He burned up all his money and he went to Alaska and it killed him. That's like: Eat shit. He had a journal and didn't he document that he was, like, dying? 'I ate some berries. Puked up my food.' I don't like the ending of the movie. I wish he'd found a bigger purpose, and uh, *Happiness is only real when shared*—that's the message he left. You know, I actually think about that an awful lot, like, What the fuck is our purpose in life? Why am *I* here? I always think about some little kid being like, 'What'd you do with your life?' And me being like, 'Well, I sold a bunch of floors.' It's like, What the fuck? You know? But then I think about everyone else who has an even more meaningless job. Imagine selling stocks and bonds. Or imagine the guy who sells olive oil." He picks up a plastic bottle of oil. "It's like, 'It was a fine life in the mountains. The winter of '72 was a whammy.'"

Then, to clarify, Bjarki says that what he's just said about telling a kid you spent your whole life slinging lumber is actually something an old Wood Mill employee once said to *him*.

Mr. Crowley, below me, is bridging the rungs of my stool.

I say, "But it's unclear to me *what* Chris McCandless was running from."

McCandless was a white, upper-class, college-educated kid.

"Mr. Crowley's actually the more snuggly one once you get him to trust you. He's trying so hard to be your friend, but he's, like, not sure of himself."

"My cat has a pink nose too."

How we are able to talk like this, I have no idea.

I say, "When I watched *Into the Wild* this time, I was like, 'This is a *sad* movie.'"

"Who was the girl?"

Kristen Stewart—another *Chris*.

"Yeah, and she dated the guy from *Twilight* and then she became a lesbian."

"Just the loneliness is so brutal to watch, dude. And now, with me and B—oh, motherfucker. I don't want to run away from people. I want to share my happiness."

"I don't know. I run away from everybody, so—"

As soon as he says it I know it will go in The Book, but in the moment I don't know how to proceed, like conversationally, like how to keep the connection going, if that's what is happening in the kitchen—genuine human connection, I mean—and so I just wait to see if he'll say something more, but he doesn't, at least not about running or not running, and the next thing I know he's showing me a video. It's less than three minutes long. The lizard stands before a forest, speaking in this outrageous Long Island accent. He's got square teeth and bumpy green skin, a very red mouth. Maybe the lizard looks smug, his arms folded, his head rolling around.

What is this? Oh, I'm king of the trees, I'm the tree-meister.

A teepee appears. A headdress. The lizard says offensive things. *Who's chair is that? Who brought that goddam chair here—that's not my chair.* There's a little kid, some balloons, some knots, some made-up words.

Who paid for that floor? Not me. No way!

I can't help myself. With each successive viewing, I see more and more meaning and connection, feel my delusion becoming real, go slightly more bonkers.

I say, "Dude, *I'm* the tree-meister." The thing is, though, when I hear myself on these recordings later, I always sound so ridiculous. It's like seeing yourself in a photograph, I guess. The way you look in the photo—it's never how you

think you look, though sometimes you look better than you think—more attractive maybe, or less tired, younger, hipper, happier, though of course it's true too that sadness also has its appeal. So—what?—maybe one in ten photos, or one in a hundred actually seems to reveal you as you think of yourself, which may or may not be a *realer* or *truer* you, like a more empirically accurate representation of who you actually are or whatever. Of course, the photographer has something to do with all of this too.

"Bjarki!" I say. "I'm writing about trees and chairs and floors and balloons and knots and Indians! *I'm* writing about *reality*!"

And Bjarki, he doesn't even say that none of that is connected to anything. He says, "Who knows why it's a lizard telling the story?")

SEVEN

M. Americana

1.

Myke Bartholf and his wife, Sue, whom Myke calls Ma, greeted us at the door. It was an early morning in March of 2017, before that first rangoon, back when I thought I'd have Bjarki figured out in no time, back when, apparently, I believed that people, like floorboards, like marriages, like secrets, like *everything*, could be figured out, and that figuring people and things out was important—imperative even, in order to connect with them and then write about them or love them or whatever. Bananas—that was something B had taken to saying, not about me in particular, not necessarily. Mango was the name of Myke and Ma's dog. The plan, which was to go ice fishing, hadn't come about because I particularly enjoy ice fishing or even because I particularly *wanted* to ice fish, but because Bjarki had invited me along and I thought some kind of prompted excitement might serve as a convenient narrative backdrop for my magazine-style essay, a bizarrely contradictory notion considering that in the realm of recreational activities, ice fishing has always seemed to me to be one of the slowest and dullest, existing mostly as an occasion to sit around and make up, or at least exaggerate, stories, which—making up and exaggerating stories—it occurs to me, is maybe what we're all doing all the time.

"Aw, I'd rather be in a position to take clothes off," Myke said. "I'm a child of the sixties." We were pulling on insulated coveralls beside a glowing woodstove. Myke, born in Florida, has a hint of southern accent and calls Bjarki, *Beej.* Glinting gold zippers slanted over his chest pockets. His grin, set in a weathered face below shaggy gray hair, was wide and crooked and contagious and he seemed capable of winking without committing an eyelid. Not often does one encounter this quintessential twinkle, but there it was.

"Myke could sell shit to an asshole," one Wood Mill employee will tell me later.

"I will sling a little B.S.," Myke says.

He pulled a brimless, leather, fur-lined hat over his ball cap and secured it with a strap beneath his chin. We went out to the porch.

Every winter afternoon for the past fifteen years, two dozen or so white-tailed deer have stopped by Myke and Ma's in anticipation of the dinner that Myke unfailingly disburses: pellets of corn and oats and barley and molasses. As a result, these Deer Run deer are not your ragtag mid-March ungulates. Their gray coats are rich, their postures dignified. They're royal, supermodel, one-percenter deer.

At seven dollars a day, Myke called it cheap entertainment.

"Aw, I used to be a mad dog hunter. Avid. But hell, once you start naming 'em and every damn thing else, you're through hunting 'em."

Intuitively, it made sense that feeding deer helps them survive. Biologists, however, caution against it. In the winter, whitetails rely on reserves of body fat for about 40 percent of their daily nutritional requirements. The microbiomes in their guts are finely tuned to the available browse—leaves and green shoots in the fall and, increasingly through the winter, woody twigs from maple, ash, birch, and witch hobble, as well as cedar and the occasional white pine. This gradual shift in diet allows the deer's gut to adjust to new sources of nutrition. Introducing sugary foods like corn or hay or molasses can slow digestion and cause an unsustainably acidic environment in the deer's stomach. Deer that are fed by humans are not uncommonly found starved to death, their stomachs packed with indigestible hay. In addition, fed deer "yard-up" near a food source. This not only facilitates the transmission of disease but also prevents the creation of trails through the snow that are necessary for deer to elude predators. Fed deer become coyote bait.

"I got one that's special," Myke says later. "She's eating right out of the damn bucket. She'll roll those big brown eyes up at you and I swear to god, there's something—there's a connection. It's like—You'd have to go *through* it."

He named her Asia, "because she's got an oriental look."

Ma shook her head.

Several ungulate biologists heaved in their graves.

2.

North Pond was a crow's mile or so distant from Myke's. Ringed by hills of coniferous green and leafless gray, its brilliant white surface appeared solid and flat enough to sharpen a chisel. We packed a couple dozen beers into the plastic sled behind Myke's snowmobile and Bjarki, grinning and enthusiastic, offered me the controls of the other.

Though I had been on snowmobiles before, I had never driven one. What I said was that I'd be glad to hold Bjarki's coffee, but I didn't want to drive and Bjarki, if he was bitter about it, he didn't say. He dashed his coffee in the snow and I mounted behind him. In this position, my thighs were straddling— literally *straddling*—Bjarki's torso and my chest was against his back, not so that I could feel the warmth of him or anything, but still, in a shuddering flash, I understood that I had become the biker babe to his biker dude—not that there is anything wrong with biker babes and biker dudes. In fact, I think I'd like being a biker dude, for about day, or, if I were a babe, a biker babe. This weirdness about close physical proximity is probably another reason I'm preoccupied with human connection. See, while I *do* want to be connected to you, I want that connection without touching, at least most of the time. In fact, as I adjusted my limbs and torso for maximal stability and minimal contact, I saw that I would also need to hold on to Bjarki, to physically attach myself to him.

Bjarki—the mind reader—said there were handles under the seat.

We descended slowly, through hemlock and alder and maple and birch, breathing in the fumes from Myke's sled, which was just ahead of us. The last time I'd been on a snowmobile, I'd been researching an essay about a mountain lion hunt outside of Saratoga, Wyoming. Actually, I hadn't been on a snowmobile then. I'd been in one of those four-wheeler-type vehicles, a UTV, cruising slowly from creekbed to ridgeline, hoping to cross the elusive cat's tracks in the snow, and we did too, we crossed several, though we never saw a mountain lion. On the one hand, I had been sad not to see a mountain lion, while on the other, I had not been sad that the paying hunters from West Virginia had not seen a lion, for if they had seen one, they would have shot it, and I most certainly did not want to see a lion get shot. But what dominates my memory of the hunt is the monotony of the snow and how, gradually, I'd come to feel as if I wasn't moving forward at all, but just nodding in place, like a boat at anchor, the snowy tide steadily pushing past. It was because of this, I think, that when Bjarki stopped, anticipation surged through me. I looked up half expecting some kind of synchronicity between my consciousness and The World.

The bundle of canvas and plastic in the trail had been discharged by the sled Myke's sled was towing. I picked it up—the chair—though actually, in that moment, it *wasn't* a chair, it was something in between, something unrealized. Though that's not true either. It *was* a fully realized thing. It's just that it also had the potential to be realized differently, as a chair.

"What?" Bjarki yelled.

"Juice it!" I yelled, imitating, I hoped, a casual familiarity with acceleration.

We turned onto a snowy road and then, at the edge of the frozen lake, or pond—I did not know the taxonomical difference—Bjarki again offered me the controls.

3.

A few moments later, grinning proudly, I brought the grumbling machine to a stop. Who knows why we leap or don't? Beginnings and endings have never sat well with me. But regarding Bjarki, you might say his journey to The Wood Mill began in 2011, with his reading of a magazine-style essay. The piece described DeadHead Lumber, a company specializing in the recovery of ancient logs from the bottom of Maine's lakes and rivers.

Now, though forest covers about 90 percent of Maine's 19.8 million acres, it is a very different forest from the one standing when the first Europeans began settling the coast. Today, the majority of Maine's trees are between ten and seventy-five years old, whereas in pre-settlement days, only about 15 percent were that young. The majority then were between 150 and 300 years old and almost 30 percent had been standing for longer than that.

Though Europeans had cleared only ten thousand acres of Maine's forest by 1760, by 1850, a million acres were being felled each decade. On November 20, 1833, the Bangor *Republican* boasted that "Maine furnishes about three-fourths of all the white pine lumber exported from the United States." The mills only stopped when the millstreams turned to ice in December. Bangor boomed into the logging capital of the world. About a billion board feet of logs were driven down the Penobscot and about 10 percent of them sunk. This was enviable wood. The slow-growing, straight-grained trees had been harvested from forests that, for ten thousand years, had been untouched by a logger's saw. Trees—and therefore logs—like these can't be found in today's forests.

Bjarki and Josh Saltmarsh, best friends and sailing teammates in college, had always talked about starting a business. They drew up plans for a barge. They sought out a sawyer to cut recovered logs into boards and they sought out a kiln to dry the boards and a planer to plane them smooth. Without any experience in the wood industry, without any vocabulary, without knowing even a fraction of what they *wanted* to know—except everything—they were laughed at and hung up on.

Myke, however, was different.

"Myke was like, 'You boys clearly don't know anything. Why don't you come on up here?' He gave us a big tour."

The friends never did haul up a waterlogged log. They bought The Wood Mill instead.

Myke stuck a hook through a shiner. When the first flag went up, Bjarki rocketed to it. He took the line gingerly in his fingers and pulled up a fish the size of an apple slice. The sun splintered on the white perch, which, in fact, wasn't a *perch* at all, but a member of the bass family, *Moronidae*: *Morone americana*.

Above us, a bald eagle, as only, it seemed, a bald eagle could, soared past, soaring.

Then not much continued to happen until Joe showed. Joe was an old rodbuster buddy of Myke's, big and funny, with hands like splitting mauls. In the winter, when concrete and steel work slowed, Joe hired himself out to shovel roofs. Recently, he'd been on top of a bottled water company just west of Auburn. Maybe you've heard of it?—Poland Spring sells around $600 million worth of bottled water a year. However, according to a recent lawsuit, "Not one drop" of Poland Spring water actually springs from a spring. The lawsuit contends that the original Poland "spring" hasn't been a spring for fifty years and that the company has instead created six "phony, manmade 'springs.'" Nestlé, the owner of Poland Spring water, counters that "Poland Spring Brand natural spring water is just what it says it is—100 percent natural spring water." (In March of 2021, Nestlé will sell all that water to a pair of private equity firms for $4.3 billion.)

Flag up.

Joe slung a brilliant black and yellow torpedo onto the ice. I saw its wet black eyes and the strength in its tail. It was sixteen inches of *Esox lucius*, or northern pike.

"Eagle chow," Joe called it. He stomped the fish with a boot.

I'd never seen a fish stomped like that before.

"You're not supposed to be here," Joe said. "You're not what I wanted."

Myke said, "Aw, the state of Maine fucked that up."

According to Myke and Bjarki, in the 1970s, the state of Maine had mistakenly introduced to its waters millions of invasive northern pike. Now the pike proliferate, feeding on, among other things, yellow perch, trout, salmon, and *Morone americana*.

4.

I mean, I didn't look into the pike tale because I take some smug pleasure in performing the role of fact-checker, at least that wasn't the whole reason. Right and wrong, true and false, fact and fiction, those neat dichotomies occupy places too disparate on some imagined moral hierarchy. People are right and wrong all the time. Good for them. Except that I *did* care if Myke and Bjarki were right or wrong. In fact, I wanted them to be *wrong*, but not because I wanted to feel superior or whatever. In those years—*those years!*—I was desperate for evidence that the government could be trusted not to accidentally introduce some kind of mega-predator into a defenseless ecosystem. But then again, I also definitely wanted Myke and Bjarki to be *right*, because then it seemed like I'd have just come across a pretty killer story for my *next* magazine-style essay. On the other hand, I also wanted them to be *wrong*, because if the subjects of my magazine-style essay were unreliable, then that might really complicate things, in a *good* way. Concurrently, though, I definitely wanted them to be *right*, because if they were *wrong*, then their unreliability might really complicate things, in a *bad* way. Of course, I also wanted Bjarki and Myke to be right because, despite my pretense of journalistic objectivity, I didn't want to prove them wrong and by so doing give offense. But then again, even if they *were wrong*, it wouldn't really be *them* that were wrong. It would just be *the information* that was false, which I think means the information wouldn't even be information, but rather gibberish—whatever *gibberish* means.

5.

Myke still had not caught a fish.

"You want a lesson?" Bjarki said.

Myke said, "Education is important, but fishing is more importanter."

To the south, you could just make out the buildings of the Pine Tree Camp, where, in 2013, the North Pond Hermit had been apprehended stealing frozen hamburgers. For a quarter of a century, Christopher Knight had lived alone, in the woods, on a hill just south of here. He'd survived in a tarp encampment by stealing propane and batteries and everything he ate, candy and canned food and booze. He never slept inside. He never lit a fire, never spent a dime, never once went fishing. On the coldest nights, he described his body entering a kind of torpor. It was all pretty hard to believe, but we all believed it.

"If you're a human," Myke said, "you're a little bit *off*."

It was uncomfortable to imagine Christopher Knight in jail.

"In a cage," Bjarki said.

6.

In the sixteenth century, a kind of northern El Dorado was rumored to exist in what is now Maine. The city, or region—it was both—mostly referred to as Norumbega, first appeared on a sparsely illustrated map in 1529 as "Oranbega." A palace stands at the confluence of two rivers. There are hills and mountains and several towering stands of pines. In the 1540s, Jean Alfonse described in his *La Cosmographie* a "city called Norombegue with clever inhabitants. . . . The people use many words which sound like Latin and worship the sun, and they are fair people and tall." David Ingram, an English sailor who, in 1567, reportedly shipwrecked near Mexico and then eventually made it to Maine, later claimed to have walked the pearl-paved streets of Norumbega. He made no mention of pines. Women wore gold necklaces and gold bracelets and golden plates like armor. By that time, England had been largely deforested for centuries. It was in desperate need of lumber, not only for building and heating homes but especially for the Royal Navy. The tall, straight, strong, light, and flexible pine trees on that first map were as good as gold. In 1584, an advisor to the Queen arguing for colonization noted "excellent trees for masts . . . to build ships and to make great navys."

"Norumbega," the advisor suggested, "offreth the remedie."

I suppose every geography, every age, every story, every relationship, every-*thing*, promises something, in a way. To get to Bjarki's boxy, metal-clad house you drive dirt roads past a couple collapsing barns, a silo askew, several tilting gravestones. In summer, an orange fox might run so straight and so fast across the road that it seems to do so without touching the ground. There are the remnants of orchards and a dam for a long-gone gristmill and hand-lettered signs advertising EGGS and NO TRESPASSING and hay fields and abrupt hills and woods and clear-cuts and trailer homes and modular homes and old farmhouses and meth houses and pot grow houses and overgrown RVs and the wagon and manure tracks of Amish travel and brilliant white turkeys in the moonlight and wild turkeys patrolling the dawn and a bow hunter draped in twigs and leaves walking the drainage ditch, a baseball diamond, a water tower.

Three winters after ice fishing, I'm at Bjarki's house listening to the Grateful Dead on vinyl singing "Sugaree." B was my introduction to the Dead. We had favorite songs.

"It *was* scary," Bjarki says, describing when Josh left The Wood Mill in 2016. For nearly a decade, the two friends had been inseparable, first living together in Rhode Island and New York City and then again in a cabin on Myke's land. They shopped together, carpooled, skied, worked, double-dated. In the end, Josh left to start a family. Bjarki bought him out.

"We were hoping to make The Wood Mill into a million-dollar business and then flip it."

Up until now, I've heard Bjarki say that he dreamt of selling The Wood Mill, but never that he purchased it with *the intention of selling it for a profit*, which seems like a big deal, like either a big omission on his part or a big failure on mine. I mean, I've meticulously documented his T-shirts (Woodstock '69, blue) (the Statue of Liberty and the words I'M WITH HER, blue) and what he ordered for breakfast and what was on the radio when he ordered (two waffles with strawberries and whipped cream, and something about *redneck girls like me*) and the small U.S. flag on the hemlock post beside us. I know about how, as a toddler, he stopped breathing and was life-flighted to a hospital and I know about how, in college, during his second summer working in China, he had that nasty ear and respiratory thing. (That infection, he says—you may have noticed it—that's why his breathing sometimes sounds a little funny.) There was the government control and the Terracotta Warriors and, of course, the Wall. During the Olympics, when he traveled to Beijing, an elderly woman approached him, begging. Maybe he gave her a little money or maybe not; the point is, you can see the horror on his face when he tells the story, as if he's to blame for what happened next. A couple blocks away, he saw the very same woman, down a side street or alley or whatever. She was being beaten by two police officers. And Bjarki—he thought it was happening because of *him*, because the woman had approached *him*. "He always cared," Bjarki's mother, Sybille, told me. (This was in Rhode Island.) Bjarki was driving the family's Sequoia SUV, which Bjarki calls a *truck*. "He cared for everybody. He was a quiet child who covered his shyness with aloofness." Sybille explained how Bjarki had learned to sail at the age of six on a small boat called an Optimist and how sailing "makes kids very independent very fast. You're in charge of your own boat. He would pull the strategy. He would always think things through and know exactly where he was going."

She said, "He wouldn't climb a tree unless he knew his way down."

He didn't play Monopoly for fun. He played to win.

"Do you know what's amazing to me," Bjarki said as he drove. "These stone walls—how each stone is perfectly stacked. Like, how did farmers a hundred and fifty years ago have time to stack perfect stone walls?"

I didn't say anything. The seats were either leather or fake leather or something that wasn't even pretending to be leather but that I mistook for leather. I mean, you'd have to be some kind of monster to find someone else's amazement repellent. To be repelled by the way they breathe. Maybe it was all just a question of hydration and blood sugar, or maybe I thought stone walls were irrelevant, or maybe I saw Bjarki's amazement as a guilelessness born of privilege—not that privilege is necessarily a bad thing. In fact, on any other day (though I'm not sure *which* day), a lack of guile might seem wondrous to me, the best manifestation of saintliness. A kid falls in love with a butterfly. Then what happens? Innocence may be a kind of freedom, but it also takes courage. My therapist, she says we react to the versions of ourselves that we see in The World, and I agree, but the Aquarian in me—without too much of a stretch, I think you can say that we *only* see versions of ourselves in The World, whether we like it or not, and so whatever it is I notice probably has something to do with *me*, though who knows *what*. I mean, I think I resented Bjarki's guilelessness because I felt implicated by it. It's incredibly narcissistic, I know, but in that moment, I felt responsible for whatever pain he might encounter because of this lack of guile, as if it was my duty—*my duty!*—to toughen up that younger version of myself, to warn him—to catch him, as it were, before he went off the cliff. Sheesh. It's amazing, how perfectly stacked our feelings are inside of us. I mean, of course The World is not a Waldorf Safe Zone, though of course I *wish* it was. (*A part of you wishes*, my therapist says.) (*Monster*, she says, *belongs to a young part*.) And on top of that, I *know* I resented Bjarki's guilelessness because it seemed to contradict the understanding I had of him as crafty-wind-reading-Monopoly-champion-business-flipper, while at the same time it *supported* the understanding I had of him that day ice fishing, as a well-fed deer outsmarted by a wily old coyote, which meant I both *had* and *had not* figured him out, which, at least at that point, seemed like a totally incoherent proposition. I mean, even as I knew Bjarki was as far beyond my comprehension as any nebula, I wished he was simpler, which, at some level, was sort of like resenting all those parts of *me* that I felt complicated who I was, or at least *some notions* of who I was, which didn't feel great. I mean, we all wall off parts of ourselves (*Exile*, my therapist says.), and I suppose I could be grateful for the opportunity to see those walls—the opportunity for self-understanding, but often I am not. In the truck-that-was-really-a-gas-guzzling-SUV, I was angry because I didn't want to be reminded of my own separation from the more guileless aspects of myself and to reassert my aloofness, I recited a little Frost. I mean, in the back seat with the leashes and the water dishes for the dogs that were not there, I *imagined* reciting a little Frost.

Something there is that doesn't love a wall.

And then I imagined the approximate opposite: *Something there is that loves a wall.*

And then I imagined that both statements were true.

And then I imagined myself to be happy.

7.

"He was a year ahead of me and he kind of took me under his wing. We were really good at shutting down our own business ideas, which is funny because then we ended up buying The Wood Mill. My theory is that he enjoys playing devil's advocate. And I'm not saying he's wrong, or right, but in college, obviously, he could get people riled up. He spent a lot of time on the internet reading contrary news sources. It snowballs. In Mercer, I watched his views get stronger and more extreme. You've probably gathered that he thinks the government is coming for him. And I don't think he's *wrong*, but. . . . There was this guy who lived across from The Wood Mill—he was like the head of the Maine Militia. He owned a tank. Like a full-on *tank*. His cellar was packed full of food and weaponry. Bjarki was into that, being prepared. He started collecting guns. He had quite the collection by the time I got out of there."

"If Bjarki could be an adjective, that'd be great. He's just Bjarki. There's no ego. We've never dated, but we're very compatible. If Bjarki chooses to be in your life, he's very present. He told me that his dad always asked him, 'What are your goals for this month and for the next six months, and how will you achieve them?' He was always thinking ahead, planning, figuring out the next step. In college, he was the instigator for—maybe not *bad* ideas—but *fun* ideas, shenanigans. I don't know if Maine is *changing* him. Personality-wise, he's mellowed, but he still has the same ridiculous streak. He called me last week to see if I wanted to be his date at his cousin's wedding in Iceland—he's very spontaneous. He would think nothing of buying a wood mill in the middle of Maine and taking up something he's never been interested in. Still, I would like to see him out of Mercer. I think he's lonely. I *know* he's lonely up there."

"He always liked helping people. Older folks, 'You need a hand? I'll do it.' Of course you wish that *everybody* would be that way and they are not. Running a business, getting disappointed by really lowlife people—sometimes he gets pretty extreme in his views. Like, whoa, where did that come from? He said to me, 'I am working my butt off and other people just take. They just suck on the system.' He has always been a black-and-white person. No gray zone. I can see his point in the small things; it's just when it comes to big politics we butt heads. But you love your child and respect your child and everyone has to find their own way."

"B was a kind and thoughtful young man. He liked listening. He liked speaking with conviction and certainty. After having him in class, we kept up on social media. Many of his comments were crass and rude, not to mention misinformed (to put it nicely). He told me he was making a million dollars and had *x*-many employees. I was happy for him, but put off. Then last month he reached out about your book. Also, I wouldn't confuse having 'no ego' with having no self-confidence. B had a lot of intellectual confidence. There might also have been some physical insecurity. He was very thin. He was a bit of a loner who could be empowered as a maverick when he was talking philosophy and politics—when he was in his realm."

8.

"Find me someone in their thirties who wants to move to bumfuck Maine and spend a million dollars to make fifty grand a year." Bjarki's talking about how difficult it will be to sell The Wood Mill.

The Dead have stopped singing. The record is still.

Well, I say. It sounds to me, Bjarki, that the ideal buyer you're describing sort of like your savior or whatever is actually *you*, which is basically what every old wise man would say, and Bjarki, he laughs because, Yeah, he knows, and we're both kind of grinning at the image of him waiting for a version of himself to walk through the door he walked through eight years ago when, oddly, or coincidentally, or meaningfully, or unbelievably or whatever, at that moment, behind him, I see the back of him standing in the sliding glass door. I can see two of him now, or both sides of one of him, front and back, which either is or isn't quite symbolically congruent with what he's telling me and is just an image in glass and beyond glass with no bearing on anything at all, and though I'm feeling pretty good because of the beer and how wise I think I sound, I'm also feeling a bunch of other stuff too, about my own walls and cages and Norumbegas and—I don't know—It sounds so moronic now, what I say next.

"So, what the fuck?" I say. "Are you trapped here?"

I'm not thinking about how our ice fishing trip ended, but I will later—I am, I mean—as I write this. I see the perch and the northern pike and the magazine-style essay frozen stiff on the ice, succeeding as dead fish, failing as eagle bait. I see the strong and dainty ungulates at Myke's cabin, ducking for the pellets of feed in the snow. When we gather inside around the woodstove, I lean against a doorjamb. Bjarki and Ma stand nearby. Myke sprawls in a recliner and Mango jumps atop his chest, licking his face like an ice-cream cone. We are flushed from the cold and the heat and the morning beer and Myke's face is shining. You can feel the cooling saliva, the hot rough of Mango's tongue, and as Myke's chuckles turn to hacking laughter, we are all laughing, laughing so hard that tears are streaming down our faces, and Bjarki, at his house, in answer to my question either now, or three years later, or whenever *this* is—he says, "Sort of. You know. For sure."

EIGHT

Shavings (Monster)

Bjarki says, "If the phone rings, pardon me, I got to grab it."

It's the end of summer 2019. I'm thirty-seven now.

I say, "I don't really—I kind of have a *DNA* thing."

"Yeah."

"You know?"

"Janet Jackson got pregnant at, uh, what, forty-eight? It's like, age is just a number."

I say some true things that feel sad to say and then I don't say some sad things that feel impossible to say and Bjarki nods and, attempting to lift my spirits, reminds me of one of the last times he and I saw each other, almost a year ago, at a reading I gave in a little art gallery.

"You're famous," he says. "You gave me your book!"

The book was a small chapbook. My voice shook. What I'm working on now is different.

"I told Nate and he's like, 'A *book* book?' And I'm like, 'That's what Matthew told me!' And Nate's like, 'He's going to be the next J. K. Rowling. It's going to be a million-dollar franchise and I need book number three,' and I's like, 'Why number three?' And he's like, 'Well, Matthew's gonna wanna keep number one and you're gonna get number two.'"

I say, "My agent is reading the first hundred pages right now."

"*Agent?*" Bjarki is as surprised as I am.

The fact is I don't have an agent, though I have been corresponding with someone who is *an* agent. He's just not *my* agent. Actually, I think he *isn't* even an agent. He's just someone who works at an agency, who could *become* an agent someday, perhaps even *my agent*. But all that aside, maybe to avoid any conversational backsliding, or maybe to prolong this exuberance or maybe just to boost my credibility, I tell Bjarki about a specific scene in The Book that I've been working on recently.

It was a Friday afternoon at The Wood Mill, just after closing. The five of us were standing around the bed of the company pickup scrutinizing the boat motor Bjarki and I had just retrieved from a machine shop down in Hallowell—or rather, the *pieces* of the boat motor, or *engine*, or whatever it was, or wasn't, supposed to be. It was just hunks of metal to me. Bjarki said it would run on diesel. Someone said that there was diesel and then there was all the rest. The boat, Bjarki said, would be named *Rolling Coal*.

He had recently turned thirty and, on our drive to Hallowell and back, he'd reflected that after six years in Mercer, he was now an "F-bomb-dropping machine." He seemed sort of proud of this, though he also said he was tired of talking about hydraulics and hunting and women all the time. Like, he wouldn't mind a little intellectual conversation once in a while. Like, in that email I'd sent, I'd used a good word! What was the word?

The email was from four days prior, September 24, 2018, 5:53 PM

Hey Bjarki:

It's been a long time since we've been in contact. I have not forgotten about you or The Wood Mill or your generosity, but the vicissitudes of this existence have preoccupied me over the past 12-16 months. So,
1. I hope you and Myke and Nate and The Wood Mill et al. are well.
2. Come hear me read in Portland on Thursday night? (I won't be reading from The Wood Mill piece, but something much more personal (flier attached).)
3. I'd like to come visit you on Friday afternoon. Maybe I could bring a few beers and we could catch up?

Be in touch,
Matthew

Et al.! That awkward mix of familiarity and formality. And those parentheses! Dear god, *flier attached*! You try your whole life not to be obnoxious and—
—Yes, he said, Yes! *Vicissitude*! He'd been at this wedding recently, and there'd been this writer there whose favorite author lived in Cuba and had

a speedboat outfitted with guns. He sounded like a real badass. Fuck, he couldn't remember his name. Who was my favorite writer?

I said that probably every white dude writer went through a Hemingway phase. I mentioned *The Old Man and the Sea,* and how recently I'd read it late into the night.

Hemingway! Yes! Bjarki remembered *The Old Man and the Sea* from high school. He hadn't really gotten it. Like, wasn't there something really deep and important going on?

I wasn't sure I *got it* either, and I wasn't sure if it mattered one way or the other. There was probably something really deep and important going on all the time.

Rylee, Bjarki's adopted border collie, had her head on my thigh.

This was when Bjarki told me that the last book he'd read was *The Catcher in the Rye,* in high school, and that he'd *hated* it.

It kind of made me sad, to hear that he hated something I loved. I was thinking about how literacy and language can be a definer of identity, a symbol of status and power, and about how in Bjarki's bluster about books, I could maybe hear an interest in me and people like me—book readers, that is—and maybe Bjarki just wanted to know more about this thing (reading) that could keep people up late into the night. I think he felt left out. And I think that because he felt left out, he felt inferior, or, maybe, more accurately, because he had never felt this power from literature, he felt that those who had felt it would judge *him* to be inferior.

"*Rylee,*" Bjarki said.

She was sitting up now, licking my cheek. It felt good to have my cheek licked.

The last time we'd all been in this truck together—me, Rylee, Bjarki—we'd been on a ferry across west Penobscot Bay bound for Vinalhaven Island. At the front of the boat, a youth baseball team in maroon jerseys was horsing around. There were two packs of pine on a trailer behind us. Not one of the boards was wider than fourteen inches and not one of them was knotless and not one of them was quite right for my magazine-style essay, and yet, there I was. It was a spectacularly clear May day, the sky a lighter blue than the ocean, white wisps of clouds, white sails, white wakes spreading behind the lobster boats racing past. Bjarki, in a pensive mood, methodically ran his fingers through Rylee's hair, feeling for ticks, which he removed, placed on the dash, and burned with a BIC lighter.

"I mean, how many kids have parents who can bankroll a company?" he said. "If I asked my dad for five million dollars right now, he'd probably give it to me. Of course, he'd want me to have a plan first. I'd probably have to sail around the world and write a book about it."

"Seal!"

People crowded to the rails and we looked too, but there was no seal that we could see. Maybe there had never been a seal. The kids were shoving each other and laughing. We were, as I've said, in a truck, on a boat, crossing the ocean to an island on planet Earth. That was a fact. That was what was happening and yet, in that moment, my awareness was not that expansive. Or maybe it was just *differently* expansive. And what is *awareness*? I was thinking about how a book, like a really good one, like the one I eventually wanted to write— someday—should never be a justification for your actions, for your life. *You* didn't need justification. You were great. Well, sure, *you* were great, but was *I* great? There was no reason not to be happy. B and I had been standing around a winter fire watching the kids in their mittens and snowsuits chasing each other. After, the road home beside the river was narrow and curving and I swear the moon was reflecting off everything that night too. We'd had our Robinson Street housewarming party by then, with all its well-wishes and compliments and tours, though I hadn't yet woken in the night to the sound of small footsteps descending from the attic. That would happen soon enough. B could care on a dime, she really could. She held me then. But I'm getting ahead of myself. I was driving us home in the small purple truck I'd bought in Wyoming shortly after we'd been married and everything outside was cold and blue and still in the moonlight. I'm sure I didn't bring it up in the best way, but what would have been the best way? We'd been guessing at everything it seemed since the beginning. In fact, later on, B told me that she had never asked for Robinson Street, which hurt, even if it was true—that she had never asked me to obsess and stress about making our perfect home, or what I imagined would be our perfect home, which meant, of course, that though the house mattered to her, other things mattered more. She could crack like a whip too.

I said, "But we *are.*"

She said, "No we *aren't.*"

Then we argued bitterly—Bjarki and I did, on that beautiful day in May after delivering those floorboards that were not twenty inches wide. We argued about sea level rise and Hillary and Putin—*Putin!*—and I didn't return to The Wood Mill for over a year when I found myself standing around with four men, sipping beers from cans, gazing at the pieces of something that, when realized a certain way, would make a boat move. All of us except for Steve were drinking PBRs. Steve was drinking a Monster Energy drink. He was an excavator operator.

The shorter, heavyset man I gathered was Turkey Tom. His navy blue T-shirt was torn oddly along the flank. In addition to being Bjarki's sometimes mechanic, he helped his family run a turkey farm. All day he'd been out chopping corn.

I didn't catch the wiry, blond guy's name. He wasn't tall either. His flannel shirt hung off him. The Marlboros he smoked were from the red pack. Recently, he said, he'd learned that his grandfather had been kind of a slut down in New Sharon. He had all these aunts and uncles down there he'd never known about. He smiled easily. Later, as I took notes about the moment, I came to refer to him as Two Teeth because voids on either side of his front teeth showed when he smiled. *Two Teeth* was just a way to identify the man, what at first glance struck me, and I don't want it to stand in for anything here, except maybe me. I'd never heard a grandfather called a slut before.

The men were looking into the truck bed talking about Ethan now, one of Bjarki's youngest employees. Ethan had never had a driver's license, but he'd just been convicted of his third drunk-driving offense. He was going to jail.

Rylee was on the truck's bench seat. Bjarki didn't want her running loose.

"I was talking to him, like, 'Man, are you going to be okay? Three months is a long time.' But he said his dad had a buddy in jail and it wouldn't be so bad."

"He was raised like that. He doesn't know anything else."

"It's either going to break him or straighten him out."

"He's fucked if it doesn't straighten him out."

"If you can't do the time, don't do the crime."

"Some guys, it's just easier to go back to jail."

"Three meals a day."

"No electric bills. No gas."

"That girl with him the other day was pretty hot, though."

"Was that the one with him when he got the DUI?"

"That was his *ex*-girlfriend."

"Man. He's always banging some new chick."

"Young chicks too."

"Smart like a retard."

"These girls are not even barely legal."

"*He's* only nineteen."

"I would have banged that chick."

"*Dude.*"

"If she was sixteen, I would have."

"They'll lock you up for talking like that."

"She's like that girl down at NAPA. You seen her? Tight little ass. Waist this big." Fingers formed a neat circle.

"She turns sideways and you can't even see her."

"I heard she told him she'd fucked her first cousin."

"Told who?"

"Ethan."

"Who?"

"The girl."

"The NAPA girl?"

"What?"

"He was telling me about it and I was like, 'Man, that's a line too far.' I mean, okay, you fuck your first cousin, but you don't *brag about it*."

"*Smart like a retard*?"

"Yeah, dumb as fuck, but hung."

"Fucking big long dick, dude."

"Like Lenny. Remember that book?"

"You didn't *read* in high school."

"Remember, though?"

"*Of Mice and Men*, right?" This was Bjarki. "Is *that* what that book was about?"

"Yeah, Lenny was this retard who banged this chick and got in trouble."

Two Teeth lit another cigarette.

"That shit will kill you," Steve said.

"So will that shit," Two Teeth said, nodding toward the Monster.

"Have you seen this video, 'Body Like a Crack Ho'?"

We watched the video.

I said I had to go, but awkwardly, because I'd never said hello.

Bjarki walked me to my truck.

"See what I mean?" he said.

I mean, I did and I didn't. I drove away feeling kind of sad. There is a photo of my five-year-old self on the dash of my truck. It's more of a reminder than a conversation piece. I'm wearing a striped shirt, cradling my belly, just as proud as anything. I'd used packing tape to laminate the picture of myself and the tape's seams kind of crisscrossed me like a grid—not that it mattered, except that I kind of wished I could see myself more clearly. *What is the grass*, the child asks. I rolled the window down. At the edge of every field, the pines were the tallest trees. I wanted to say they were head and shoulders taller. They looked yellow where the sun was on them. In shadow, a dark green. I was sad about what had been said around the truck, which was reckless and foul and mean, and I couldn't and didn't want to dismiss it as just men being men or locker room talk. It couldn't be dismissed, not really. But what I was really sad about was that the conversation I'd witnessed was all I had seen of those men, maybe all I would ever see. Our windows onto the world are small. Did it matter that Brett Kavanaugh's Supreme Court hearings were on the radio and that I turned them off? If only I'd cracked a joke or known something those men didn't know about boat motors or if I'd just asked a question, like at least what Two Teeth's name was. Or, if they liked working for Bjarki. I don't know. I don't mean for my regrets to sound exclusively journalistic—they weren't, not at all. Nor were they compassionate or redemptive, like I wouldn't have intended those questions to be an opportunity for those men to consider what maybe none of us ever really consider. I guess I wished I'd asked something, anything really, for some reassurance that I had not just spent the last forty minutes drinking from a red, white, and blue can in a parking lot all alone.

"Those were some pretty extreme characters right there."

That's true, and also not true.

"I hope that—"

I never hear what Bjarki hopes. I think he's worried about people being misrepresented in The Book, which I'm worried about too. God, I'm worried about that. But instead of saying so, instead of saying something about truth and connection, I say something dressed up and pompous and vague, something about objectivity as opposed to the *appearance* of objectivity, about how the reality we experience might not be the real reality. It's convoluted what I say.

NINE

Irreconcilable Differences

Now here's Nate Lesperance with his hat in just about everything at The Wood Mill. Not his literal hat. His literal hat is a grease-rimmed ball cap marked with the Puma logo that I've only seen him remove in order to scratch at his close-cropped hair, a vigorous gesture that seems to emphasize the determination of his thinking. Determinedly, he thinks animals are cool. He likes zoos. He does not own a gun, does not own a snowmobile, doesn't vacation, dislikes Florida. He's divorced, has two daughters and two dogs, wants to date a woman five foot seven inches tall. Basically, he says, he's a wicked go-with-the-flow guy until something bugs him. Stupidity bugs him; washing dishes bugs him; reading bugs him. "No, no, I get it. Let's just skip all that. Let's go. Move along." He says he says exactly what he thinks and as a result, a lot of people think he's a wicked dick. He, on the other hand, thinks he's relatively nice. He does impersonations, puns frequently, sends laughter spilling from him like toy building blocks. Without a tape measure, he can tell you how wide that board is, how many board feet that log contains. He discerns variations in thickness by the thousandth of an inch. One board foot is equal to one square foot of wood one inch thick. Nate's hand, from pinkie to thumb, spans nine and five-eighths inches. His thick shoulders and sloping neck cast shadows like geography. By the time a pine floorboard has left The Wood Mill, he has handled it at least three separate times. "I have an advantage, or disadvantage—call it what you want—but I know what wood looks like when it's wet and green. I know what wood looks like after it's dry and after you plane it. I can look at that frozen green board and in my mind pass it through every phase of the process. I tell people, 'We do everything from the forest to your floor.' We saw it, we stack it, we stick it, we dry it, we plane it, we ship it. I've seen so much wood, it's just, like, boom: knot, knot, knot. Boom: split. Boom: crack, check, wind shake, twist, pitch, stress, bow, junk."

It was a windy morning in January of 2019 and we were in Nate's Honda Civic about two hours north of The Wood Mill, in Chester, overlooking the

W. T. Gardner & Sons hardwood chip mill. Clouds raced across a pale blue sky. The sun passed through the car like the beam of a flashlight. Nate was eating a miniature hot dog bun stuffed with peanut butter and Fluff. Behind us, long stacks of skinny hardwood logs terraced the hillside like a series of fortifications. Skinny, in this case, meant about twelve inches at the butt. Many of the logs were marked by dark cores of rot.

"It's just junk. It's not any good. It's literally just junk."

Below us, a crane rose from a heap of chaotically arrayed logs. Imagine standing in a pile of pencils that comes up to your knees. That's the scale we're talking about here. We watched as the crane lifted a bundle of logs, swiveled, and then deposited them near a large conveyor. There were ramps and towers and a vibrating hopper, and at the end of the line, what had once been logs now flew through the air in an uninterrupted spray of chips. A bucket loader worked the edge of the chip mountain, filling a tractor trailer, which promptly departed, bound for a pulp mill where the wood chips would be broken down into wood pulp, the primary component of cardboard and paper.

Dude, I said. The physical forest becoming a physical book.

Let's not get carried away, Nate said.

"Yeah," I said. "Let's go get some Dunks."

When we'd left The Wood Mill that morning, dark earth showed through the snow around the trunks of trees. In fact, we weren't driving to Chester to look at a bunch of skinny hardwood, but so that Nate could buy one or two center-mount trucks' worth of pine logs, which would in turn be sawn into boards by The Wood Mill's occasional sawyer, Travis Marble. Because The Wood Mill is the highest-paying buyer of pine logs in the state—it pays eight hundred a thousand, or $800/1,000 b.f.—loggers *want* to sell to them. This can lead to junk logs being dressed up as gun barrels. "These local Podunk guys will take old logs and retrim the ends," Nate said. A trimmed end will make a tree felled in July appear to be a tree felled on Christmas. A guy had done this once, leaving a neat pile of sawdust at the end of each log. "*That*," Nate said, is "where the whole *stupid* thing comes in."

In industry parlance, a gun barrel log is a select grade or a veneer grade log, a smokin' log, a cream log, a hot log, and this is what Nate is after. He only wants logs cut in winter, as wide as he can get them, sixteen foot six inches long. The first six inches of a logger's tape measure are blank. A gun barrel is generally the first log cut above the stump, the section of trunk referred to as the *butt*, where the highest proportion of clear, knotless wood is found.

"The Wood Mill is so picky, it's pretty easy to grade a log," Nate said. If your log's got a big hump in it or if it's folded in on itself or if the bark is scarred from something other than a machine or if there are any old limbs visible or evidence of bugs or rot, Nate doesn't want it. Still, though *grading* is easy, it's impossible to predict exactly how the boards will saw out.

"There's a saying: A log is like a woman. She can be beautiful on the outside and—"

Myke had told me that.

Then he said, "You know, that's true and it isn't."

Trees and trees and trees went by.

I asked if there was a Dunks in Chester. I said the reason I was asking was because I had a gift card.

Nate said, "So what's the basis of the book anyway?"

The *basis*? I didn't know how the basis of The Book could be unclear to Nate at this point, considering, I thought, all the synopses I'd given over the past three years, both to Nate and to Bjarki, and considering the fact that I was—as Nate knew—researching The Book at that very moment, that we, right now, were very clearly the *basis* of The Book. One of my friends likes to say that 99 percent of all anger is anger with yourself. What bugged me wasn't really Nate's curiosity. It was my own continued inability to concisely articulate the basis of The Book—to articulate what it was *about*, as if books are ever really *about* anything, and so I basically reiterated to Nate what I'd alluded to before, to everyone, which was that the basis of The Book was The Wood Mill's wide pine boards, and pine trees, and America, and of course Bjarki, and also human connection in a polarized world—if that wasn't too much—which all *felt* true, even though I knew it wasn't, at least not completely, and even after I said all that, I still felt like Nate wasn't quite sufficiently excited about The Book, which I didn't really *need* him to be, but which I very much *wanted* him to be, and so I added, almost as an afterthought, while struggling to convey in the most un-afterthought way, because you can see how my portraying you as an afterthought might be offensive—Oh, and me and you both will probably be in there too.

"Like little blurbs in there," Nate said.

"Yes," I said. "Everyone's a blurb." See, I never know when to stop talking about The Book, especially when I'm talking with someone who is *in* The Book—that is, when *I* am in The Book, or at least when a blurb like me is living through a scene that might later exist in The Book, and so in my confusion I said something about how there was still *a fuck ton*—I said that, *a fuck ton*—of research to be done, like, for instance, how do pine trees even grow, and Nate—*unflappable Nate*, I thought—he said, "Wool, they have roots that take nutrients from the soil," which was of course true, but because of its elementary nature, I had no idea if Nate was effing with me or genuinely trying to be helpful. I have all this on tape.

Pines, Nate said, die from the outside in. "If you see a funky-ass pine, you know it's all shit inside."

What I heard Nate saying was that a pine wore no gloss, that the qualities he admired in people had been realized by the pine, except it also seemed like there was more nuance to it than that, which maybe I hadn't or couldn't fully comprehend, or like maybe he was contradicting himself—not that there's anything wrong with contradicting yourself—because hadn't he said earlier that you will *never know* a pine log's true nature until you cut into it?

We exited the highway.

In the W. T. Gardner log yard, pickup trucks were parked in a line, backed into their spaces, ready to go. There were two green metal-sided warehouses and several covered tractor trailer bays. A radio tower towered over the buildings and the surrounding trees, which were young and mostly hardwood, devoid of leaves. As Nate maneuvered his Honda down an icy slope, the logs came into view. There were five rows, each row about five hundred feet long. There were logs a full forty-eight feet long and logs cut to sixteen and a half feet. Hardwood and softwood. Lumpy pine logs, sweepy pine logs, gun barrel logs, more logs than I had ever seen in one place. For a moment, I stood them all up in my mind, a forest.

"See. See those. Those are perfect."

"See all the funk on the bottom of that one."

"Junk. I'm not touching those."

"Ooooh! That thing is monstrous! Sometimes I'll buy a big one just for fun."

We got out of the car and shuffled over the ice. A truck idled nearby. Mounted to its long flatbed was a swiveling cab with a knuckle boom, and hitched behind that was something resembling a boat trailer bisected by a circular saw blade. The blade was five feet in diameter and spinning. It was called a *slasher*.

A paunchy man got out of the truck. Under an oak-patterned ball cap, Robbie wore glasses with rectangular frames and a trim, silver goatee. A lit cigarette hung from his lips. He had on a Carhartt vest zipped over a denim shirt. His sleeves were partially rolled up.

Robbie said two words to me, "I'm married," and I laughed because I didn't get the joke.

Nate inspected two pine logs lying parallel to the road. One might have been thirty inches across; the other was more like twenty-four. A young pine tree has smooth, waxy bark. On the larger log, fissures in the bark an inch or so deep separated the blocky scales that were composed of layers and layers of flakes, like books of solid phyllo dough. At first, the bark seemed a uniform gray, but it was not one color at all. There were darker and lighter grays, something close to black, vague violet hints, deep muddy browns, and where the scales had been abraded, there were reds and oranges and rusts. Green lichen hands waved from the bark. Green lichen beards hung from the bark. Bark is armor, a rustproof raincoat and fireproof gear, insulation and skin. It grows continuously, from the inside. The oldest bark is the bark closest to you, unless you are inside the tree. Where are you? At one end of the log, buttresses flared from the trunk. Icy snow clung to the darker, star-shaped whorl at the cut's center. *Whorl* is pronounced *whirl*. A pine produces branches annually, radiating from the trunk at a single elevation, often in whorls of five. You can count the number of whorls on a young tree and know its age. You can look at the vertical space between whorls and know how much height a tree gained in a given year. Hammer a nail into the trunk of a pine. Upon your return, seventy-five years later, the nail will appear to have vanished. This will not be because the nail has ascended fifty feet with the growth of the tree, but because the tree, expanding its circumference, has subsumed the nail. Unlike a human, a tree only grows taller at the tips of its branches, the topmost of which is called the *leader*. The whorl we were looking at was the encased remains of the tree's first branches.

"Most woods," Nate said, "have been picked over for good pine. In the past five years, size has dwindled drastically. The stuff that I bought last year, say, averaged twenty-two inches or less, but five years ago, it was twenty-four to twenty-five inches."

To estimate the age of a white pine in Maine, measure its diameter fifty-four inches from the ground. This is the diameter at breast height, or DBH. In general, trees of the same species growing in particular zones, grow at predictable (averaged) rates, which are approximated by a growth factor. The product of a tree's GF and DBH is equivalent to the tree's age. The GF of the eastern white pine is 5. The math for a twenty-four-inch-diameter pine tree, the minimum diameter required to make one of those twenty-inch-wide boards, necessitates a tree older than any human being who has ever lived, a tree about 125 years old.

Though Nate had the hood of his sweatshirt up over his hat, the top half of his coveralls hung from his waist. The wind swatted the dangling fabric torso.

I said, "Are all these logs butts?"

Robbie said, "I like big butts."

Nate said, "I'm a big butt guy. I'm a sucker for a good butt."

It was as if I had set them up, but I hadn't. You asked a serious question and got, it seemed, a serious joke, except I couldn't tell if these men *were* joking, or if they were serious, or both. I figured they were talking about women, but they could just as well have been talking about logs or dudes or whatever. And maybe they actually did enjoy and have some fondness for big butts (people, logs, whatever) and maybe they felt compelled to share that fact. That seemed fine. In any case, they clearly had rapport and I felt welcomed by their banter.

"You're not going to put me in your dossier, are you?" Robbie asked.

"Of course I am," I said. "You're the boss."

"The Boss Hog," Robbie said, rubbing his gut.

Again I laughed because I did not understand.

With a black crayon, Nate placed several large *WM*s on the ends of several logs.

"A *crayon*? I can't see a crayon!" Robbie short-stepped across the ice to retrieve a can of marking paint. "If I fall down, are you going to laugh at me?"

"Fuck yeah, man." Nate said. He said the three words as if they were one: *Fuckyeahman.* "I love it when people fall. But I will help you up."

Robbie sprayed the end of each log with red paint. Then he curled against the wind and lit a cigarette. He wanted to know if Nate had a new woman yet.

"Nope."

"Good man."

"They're all *nuts.*"

"So you're just fucking them all, ain't ya?"

"Trying."

"How's your daughter? She had an ear infection the last time I saw you."

"She's in school today."

Robbie nodded. The men cursed and thanked each other and then we left.

We drove past the log yard of H. C. Haynes and the Treeline log yard and then, perhaps following up on the conversation we'd had earlier, Nate said, "Yeah, I'm not a big reader."

He told me why.

"Too *descriptive*," I repeated, exaggerating the syllables as I wrote in my notebook.

"And slow-moving."

"And. Slow. Moving."

The car's seat belt alert beeped.

"This is what I tell people: reading ruins the movie for me." He was enjoying himself. "You know how people see a movie and they're like, 'The book was so much better!'? Well, it's like, I *didn't* read the book and I thought the movie was *fucking awesome*. I'm sorry that reading *sucked* the enjoyment out of your life."

I said, "I think this car is telling you to buckle up."

I said, "Is that what that beeping is?"

I said, "Sorry."

I was feeling slightly threatened, not physically—though I'm sure Nate could basically delimb me—but more like existentially. I mean, I don't think Nate judged the fact that I was writing a book—"to each his own," I've heard him say—but I think Nate didn't understand what actual *good* writing a book did, especially a book about a floor. I think he regarded books as sacred or magical objects (which they sort of are), though I'm not sure he would have said it like that, and I think he thought a book's specialness shouldn't be wasted—*wasted*, that's my word—on ordinary people or whatever kind of person he thought himself to be. Of course, there is a long history of ordinary people, of working-class people, of peasants, farmers, miners, seamstresses, of people without lots of books in their lives, appearing in books, and so perhaps Nate was concerned with literature's expectation that these ordinary people not only toil bookless in their ordinary lives but also somehow toil in a book in order to connect a reader to a more authentic, *realer* reality —The Truth. You see, from one perspective, you could say that authors (and readers) are attracted to ordinary people not because they (authors and readers) are interested in social or literary justice (ordinary people), but because they (authors and readers) want to *appear* interested in justice, because this appearance of interest marks the author as good (making the world a better place by "humanizing the other" (connection)) and, by extension, marks a reader as good (making the world a better place by "seeing the other as human" (connection)), and, by extension, makes money. Or, from a slightly different perspective, you could say that a book is like a zoo and the reader is like a zoo-goer. Are zoos good for the animals? Are they good for the world? For the zoo-goer? The ethics of it is pretty complicated, potentially. In addition, in the car, I sensed that Nate might also think that *my* time would be better spent doing carpentry (ordinary things) full-time instead of doing carpentry not-quite-full-time while also writing—or in my case, *trying to write*—The Book. And I *got* that. It was easy to see how installing a floor was more useful than writing *about* a floor. Or maybe that was just my own insecurity projected, and what I perceived as aggression from Nate was really just a guarded curiosity about me—that what I felt as a threat was actually an attempt at connection.

"*I'll* read stuff—I will. But, a regular book? That drives me nuts."

I clarified what a regular book was.

"Obviously, because it's a book, it *has to be descriptive*, but, ugh! 'A guy walks into a *dank, dimly* lit room. A lamp *flickers* in the corner.' It's like, I don't fucking care! What's the dude doing in the room? But—" Nate often employs prepositions like punctuation. "You know, I know *how to read*. It's not like I can't or I'm not smart enough. I just choose not to."

I was laughing now, but uncomfortably—very uncomfortably—because it felt like Nate thought that I thought that he was illiterate, which I definitely did not think. And even if he was illiterate, so what? I mean, not *So what* like literacy and illiteracy don't matter, but *So what* like I wasn't going to judge him either way. Literacy was a gift, I thought, like sight. Or a curse, I thought, like sight.

Of Mice and Men was one book Nate remembered thinking was okay. "To this day, if someone acts a certain way, I'll call them Lenny. I'll go, 'Okay there, Lenny.' And certain people are like, 'Oh my god. That's awesome. And mean.' That's the thing, there's a lot of Lenny's out there. I don't even *know* how certain people function. I try to go through life not getting help, if I can. But everyone needs help at certain times, borrowing money or doing this, doing that. But why should I go out of my way to help someone who is being stupid. I used to—"

He sighed.

"I remember reading *Ethan Frome*. I read the *whole* fucking thing. And I remember thinking that his wife was such a bitch. What's her name, Zeena? So then we read *The Scarlet Letter*. That was the most boring book! I was like, 'Fuck this,' and I quit reading and I got a seventy-two on the test! I'd gotten a thirty-something on the *Ethan Frome* test and I'm like, 'Doubled my score? Didn't have to read? Win, win. We're gonna do that.' And that was the end of reading."

We pulled into the chip mill yard and Nate ate his peanut butter and Fluff and I said the thing about the literal forest becoming a literal book and then we got on the interstate.

"You can get your fix in thirty-four minutes," Nate said, reading from his GPS.

"I've got this Dunkin' gift card." I'd forgotten I'd already said that.

Nate said, "I love gift cards."

Gift cards, I understood, had nothing to do with anything, but since we were on the subject, I said I'd also received a gift card to a Shaw's supermarket, and Nate was like, "Here's the thing: Does Shaw's *sell* gift cards? Because I get Hannaford gift cards and I'm like, 'Fuck yeah, man! Free groceries!' Or, *depending*, I might decide to use the Hannaford gift card to get *another* gift card, like for Longhorn, and then it's like, 'Sweet. Now I can go out for free!'"

Croissan'wich, I wanted to say, because that was a word I really liked, and I thought that if I shared something that I really liked it would multiply the effect of Nate's enthusiasm for gift cards, an enthusiasm that was contagious and a joy to be around, even though I'd never been to a Longhorn and the Dunkin' gift card in my wallet had been a gift from my wife's parents (my wife, B, whom I'd recently separated from, or with. In fact, shortly after we'd left The Wood Mill that morning, Nate had told me that *he* was divorced. "We were sitting on the couch and I was like, 'Hey let's do the forms online.' She was grading papers and I was watching a movie. Nine years we were married. Everyone says 'irreconcilable differences,' which, wouldn't that always be the answer? Like, obviously. Then we go in front of the judge and the judge is like, 'There's a two-week waiting period, or you can sign today and you're divorced.' We signed. The judge is like, 'I want to commend you. This has been the easiest divorce case ever.'"

I said, "Yeah, my wife and I are separating."

According to my Voice Memos app, we'd been driving for fifteen minutes.

"So why are you getting divorced, if you don't mind me asking?"

"We're not getting *divorced*."

The hope, I said, is that The Separation will reconcile what has *seemed* irreconcilable, which was true, even if I said it in a clever way.

Separation, I said, leading to *connection*.

Or the opposite, I didn't say—separation leading to separation.

And just as quickly as I felt the relief of revelation, I also felt unsure if I had actually revealed anything or, if through my cavalier tone, I had only *mis*revealed something, downplaying my own personal upheaval surrounding The Separation. And it's not like anything in Nate's reaction indicated that he wasn't taking me seriously, or that he judged me, but there *was* the fear that if I continued down this road (not the literal highway) of sharing (which, I realize, I hadn't shared a lot, though it felt like a lot), then we'd inevitably get into the nitty-gritty about dryer lint and toilet seats and any one of those red-faced nights in our bright kitchen when I felt sure that the neighbors could see us.

She said, "This is what it's like to be a human."

I said, "I'm trying to understand."

She said, "You're not *listening*. You're *dismissing*."

I was sitting, cutting red peppers. Behind me, there was chicken in the skillet. I remember laughing. Then we were on our hands and knees picking up vegetables from the shining Wood Mill of Maine floor that had never once stopped insulting me. I said the broccoli didn't care. She apologized to the cucumber. And even if airing all that junk out—though maybe it's not *junk*—can be incredibly cathartic (so I've heard), I wasn't ready to go there with Nate (though maybe I should have gone there). In addition, I was feeling guilty about having just shared more with Nate than I had ever shared with Bjarki (even if I hadn't shared a lot, though it felt like a lot) and I was concerned that Nate would tell Bjarki and that not only would Bjarki feel betrayed by me but I was also concerned that he would think less of me because of The Separation. Basically, I wanted to be seen by Bjarki as unfailing and happy, as someone I wasn't, which was the opposite of how I thought I wanted to see Bjarki and Nate and The World, which I'm sure set some kind of new high-water mark for hypocrisy) and clearly, there were all kinds of feelings tied up with that gifted piece of plastic in my pocket, like how its use might serve to re*connect* me to B via the feelings of warmth and generosity engendered by a free meal, or, on the other hand, its use and disposal would serve as a symbol similar to, say, pawning my wedding ring, which, because of some past accidental collision I was never able to identify, was actually more like an oval than a ring. Life, I guess. So now, in addition to turning the silver band, I'm always pressing the top and the bottom of it, in an attempt, probably, to reverse the rotation of the Earth.

We pulled off the highway in Bangor, and I got my Croissan'wich, which was actually just a plain old croissant sandwich, because Croissan'wich is trademarked and belongs to Burger King, and Nate got a sandwich too and we both ordered meatless Beyond sausage, just to give it a try, and if I felt much of a connection or a separation to anyone—servers, Nate, B, America— I was oblivious. I thought the Beyond sausage tasted Indian and Nate thought it tasted Italian. There were, at that time, 11,300 Dunkin' stores open in 36 countries, serving more than 3 million people a day. Never mind the slaughtering feedlot reality—livestock, it turns out, account for 14.5 percent of all global greenhouse gas emissions, or an equivalent of 7.1 gigatons of carbon dioxide per year (transportation, cooling the meat, burning the rainforest, fertilizing the grain to feed the cows, cow burps, etc.). A gigaton is equal to one billion metric tons. A metric ton is equal to 2204.6 pounds. It's hard to conceptualize gas having weight, like what that would even look like, but 7.1 gigatons is roughly equivalent to the mass of 102 billion people, or about 13 times the mass of the world's human population, which numbers about 7.8 billion people. The average human, breathing about 20,000 times a day, will exhale about 2.3 pounds of CO_2. Pounds! Four to five percent of our exhales are carbon dioxide, a concentration about one hundred times greater than what we breathe in. (About 21 percent of the air we breathe in is oxygen. Seventy-eight percent is nitrogen and the rest is argon, carbon dioxide (0.04 percent), neon, helium, and hydrogen.) (The wood in a white pine tree is 49.74 percent carbon.) The reason we exhale so much CO_2 is because we use food (fats, carbohydrates, and proteins) sort of like internal combustion engines use gasoline. The carbon dioxide in our exhale is mostly the result of metabolizing food (beef, Beyond, sunlight).

"So, what else do you want to talk about?"

While Nate, it seemed, had become energized by all that Beyond, I was feeling worn out. I said I was happy to sit in silence, but that wasn't exactly true. It felt like if I didn't ask any questions, then Nate would think that *he* didn't interest me, whereas, frankly, at that point I was thinking the opposite. I was thinking that *Nate* was the wood guru I'd always hoped Bjarki would be.

NATE: I like to call it the Extension Cord Fiasco.

N: So Tyler takes the red cord and then he comes back and he's like, 'I can't find the other cord.' (Tyler is, or was, The Wood Mill's youngest employee. I've never met him.)

N: I go, 'If I find it, I'm going to be pissed. Because it means you didn't look.'

N: I go, 'What the *fuck*?'

N: I go, 'Holy shit, man.'

N: So he goes to Bjarki and says, 'Nate's being a dick. I'm going home.'

N: The next day, I send Tyler a text to see if he needs a ride and he texts *Bjarki* that he's skipping work because he's mad at me and blah blah blah.

N: I wrote, I go, 'Listen.'

N: [sipping Pepsi Max]

N: I go, 'You need to man up and show up. I don't care if you're having issues at home.'

N: So he writes back, 'Oh, I know you don't care about me.'

N: I go, 'That's not *at all* what I meant.' I go, 'If you had *read* what I wrote—'

N: So he writes this whole fucking monologue.

N: I go, 'I'm not reading this.'

I was fiddling with the hot-air vents. I mean, I'm sure I *appeared* to be listening attentively, but in reality, I was failing to listen to Nate in the way I sincerely believed all people ought to be listened to. Maybe you could say I was *dismissing* him. My therapist—she says that being a good listener isn't the same as being a good sponge, the implication being that I tend toward sponge, hoping, perhaps, for total connection through total absorption, as if I can somehow soak up all the irreconcilable differences that will always exist between everyone and then—what? Probably, I think that will make the world a better place.

Nate's phone rang.

N: Is this, like, a telemarketer call?
N: Nope.
N: I appreciate your call, I do, but I am all set. Thank you. Mmm-bye. Car insurance.
N: I've yelled at pretty much everyone. What I try to do is—
N: [laughing]
N: —If I get mad, I like to get it out and get it done with and then we're good. Nothing's bothering *me*. I'm done. However you feel now is up to you.
N: My dad was a yeller. I don't want to say he browbeat you, but—when he was mad, you knew you fucked up.
N: And it's like, shit man.
N: [laughing] [little kid voice] I don't want to get yelled at.

I looked at Nate. In that particular moment, I had forgotten that Ethan sometimes affectionately calls him Dad. That he owns a blue 1968 Mustang, the first car he ever bought. That as a kid he collected comic books and Nike Air Jordans. That he says he'll read stories to his daughters all day. That on some mornings he wakes up with blurry vision that might last a couple hours until, for whatever reason, it resolves to clarity. It was like all of that stuff didn't exist and that he, like the complete metaphysical Nate, was only and exclusively the narrow-eyed Nate I saw sitting next to me. Of course, I had no idea that a year later he'd say, "If we had a planet with no people, it would just be animals doing their thing. Earth would be pretty fucking sweet." And while my understanding in the car didn't encompass that future Nate, maybe it could have been open to the *possibility* of that Nate, though I

don't know how I would have known how to predict *who* that Nate would be, like what he would be like on his metaphorical inside, if he would be better or worse—whatever that means—though maybe that's the point, that you *don't* know how someone will open up and you can't ever really *know*, about anyone, including yourself.

TEN

Shavings (Whose Fault?)

Bjarki says, "If the phone rings, pardon me, I got to grab it."

It's August 2019, 4:03 in the afternoon. The Wood Mill office opens at seven and closes at four. They're not open Saturday or Sunday. Bjarki tells me that almost a year ago, Rylee, his dog, was killed by a car on Route 2.

Bjarki says, "The dog up and died."

Nate says, "Up and died."

Bjarki says, "Are there any UPS labels?" He says the UPS guy is a pretty cool dude. Then he asks what I'm doing later and I say I'm having dinner with friends who live nearby, which is true, and he says, "Can I invite myself out with you?"

I say, "That's probably not a great idea."

Nate says, "I'm very interested in how it's *not a great idea!*"

Bjarki says, "How about *I* invite your friends out with *us*?" Which seems like an excellent conversational turn, a way to mask if he's feeling disappointed or left out or whatever. I can see why he might be. He was always inviting me to do things and hang around and, in addition, even after I'd disappeared for a year because of those vicissitudes of existence, he'd still driven all that way to support me at my little reading, and now, the *one* time he asks to do something, I say *no*.

Well, I don't actually say *no*.

I say, "My friends are swingers and we're doing a little swap."

My friends are not swingers. There's probably all kinds of Freudian stuff going on when I say that.

Nate says the whole swinging thing is going around.

He says, "We just had a hot architect in here!"

When he says *hot*, it sounds like *hut*. A hut architect.

"Nate almost picked her up!"

Nate says The Architect's last name, which none of us can really believe.

"I go, 'I'm not trying to be mean, but your name cracks me up.' She goes, 'Yeah, it's very *fitting* too.' And I look at her like, *Ahem*, throat clear. And she goes, 'My husband and I, we swing.' And I go, 'Good to know.' And she's like, 'I told my husband that there's this super hut guy down at the Mill.'"

"And she wasn't talking about me!"

"And I'm like, 'I would totally have sex with you.'"

"Is that what you said?"

"Ohfuckyeah."

"What's it called, when, um, a husband gets off to watching another guy bang his wife?"

Nate says, "Voyeurism."

I say, "There's also cuckolding."

The phone rings.

"Hold on," Bjarki says. "We got to tone this down."

The Wood Mill has been closed for nearly half an hour.

"Yeah, we have a lot of shavings right now."

"Yeah, I don't know if I could do that cuckolding stuff."

"We've probably got eighty to a hundred bags right now."

"I think I would just be enraged." That's me, saying these things.

Nate says, "*Enraged.*"

Bjarki says, "I can't say the idea has even crossed my mind."

"If I had a super-hut wife—no, she doesn't even need to be super-hut—the woman that *I love*—"

We go on like this, imagining ourselves into the bodies of strangers, except, I'm thinking, they aren't *complete* strangers—they can't be. I mean, because *we* are the ones imagining *them*, in some ways, they *are* us.

Two clowns stand at the counter. They're wearing the baggy pants, the wide yellow shoes, the red noses, the fantastic-colored wigs. They've dropped in to thank Bjarki for his donation to a fundraiser. As they leave, one of the clowns asks us the difference between an adult party and a children's party.

He blows up a long red balloon.

He ties it and twists it so that it resembles a poodle.

He squeezes the poodle.

An obscene appendage grows between the dog's hind legs.

"I love adult parties," he says.

"Dude," Nate says, "we should get Wood Mill underwear with our tree on the crotch. *Buy some wood. Get a thong.*"

Our tree is a reference to The Wood Mill's logo, a single conical conifer that is very clearly not a pine tree. No one seems to care about this even though it seems like one of those details that might undermine The Whole Book. And another thing is that when you search for The Wood Mill of Maine on Google, the first result will direct you to a page that strongly suggests that you have been infected by a virus.

Bjarki says that if you type in the proper URL, the virus thing won't happen, which is true.

Try it.

It's Election Day 2020.

Nate says, "What's a gay guy's favorite restaurant?"

Bjarki says, "Five Guys."

Nate says, "There you go!"

I say, "I should probably go put this door in."

Myke sees me and says, "Oh, no!"

Nate says, "*Oh, no.*"

The last time I saw Myke was before Covid.

He says, "I'm fully marinated."

He means vaccinated.

Nate says, "Me too!" He's not serious. "It's a little sketchy, when they're, like, bribing people. You know they're not doing it for the *greater good.*"

Bjarki says, "I heard they're giving out fifty-dollar gift cards."

"Hell, they got million-dollar lotteries. A million dollars!"

"Who's the demographic they're after with fifty dollars to Longhorn or whatever?"

"I heard it on the radio."

"You don't even know if the million dollars is *real.*"

Myke asks who brought the Dunks.

I say I get better material for The Book when I bring coffee. We are in the future now, The Afterward. The U.S. Capitol was stormed months ago. Today, I'm going to observe the last thing I need to observe in order to write The Book: twenty-inch boards passing through the planer.

Outside, the yard is ice. Menno—short and skinny, seventeen years old—is wearing insulated boots that look suitable for walking on the moon. He's been working at The Wood Mill since December. Scarcely two weeks ago, the insurrectionists stormed the U.S. Capitol.

Bjarki says that because he speaks some German, he can understand some Pennsylvania Dutch. "It's German and Dutch. Deutsche and Dutch."

I say, "Is Dutch different from Deutsche?"

Pennsylvania Dutch is what many Amish people speak across the United States, not just in Pennsylvania. It's a mashup of German and English and not particularly related to Dutch at all. Dutch is spoken in the Netherlands. You don't need a book to tell you that ignorance is a force like gravity; it makes the world go round. Holland is something else entirely.

Bjarki says, "Somebody told me that the Amish vocabulary has way less words than the English vocabulary."

"Oh. Totally."

Have I not mentioned that Nate is in the office too? He recounts a time when Menno did not understand the word *flush*. He smooths his hand across a surface that isn't there. "I go, 'You know, *even* all the way across?'"

Menno says, "Nope."

"In Amish, the same word has way more multiple meanings."

"It's like the opposite of Eskimo."

Eskimo may not actually be a language. In fact, it has been suggested that *Eskimo*, the word used by much of the world to describe the Inuit and Yupik and Aleut people living around the northern polar regions, comes from *ayaškimew*, which means "a person who laces a snowshoe." Others have suggested that *Eskimo* derives from a word meaning "a person who eats raw meat." All this naming stuff is kind of a delicate situation, potentially.

"Like *mensch*."

"Like a hundred words for ice."

"Mensch means *person*. It also means *man* and *woman*."

"What'd you say, *mensch*?"

"It's German for *human*. But they use it for anybody, like *that guy*, *that dude*. Everybody's just *mensch*."

I say, "Isn't it derogatory, in English? To call someone a mensch?"

Bjarki says, "It's just *human*."

Nate says, "*Wench*."

I say, "It seems like a stingy person is a *mensch*."

Nate says, "That's a *miser*."

Bjarki says, "Human."

Nate says, "That's a nice color blue."

A blue pickup has just pulled into the yard, driving slowly and, it seems, aimlessly.

Bjarki says, "This happens like three times a day. It's a drive-through men-sching. We always wonder, 'What did they come in for? Why didn't they stop in the office? Who are they?' They might actually be here for shavings."

A skinny man in shorts comes in wearing black PF. Flyer shoes and a hat with a flat brim. An ornate floral tattoo wraps his arm. He's carrying a six-foot length of orange-grained wood. He takes off his blue surgical mask.

Nate says, "What you got?"

Bjarki says, "Southern yellow."

"Guess again."

"Alaskan cedar."

"Red cedar."

"Inland cedar."

"Red pine."

PF. Flyer makes the sound of a bell.

What else is new?

Well, tomorrow, Nate is going to court because his dogs won't stop bark-ing—*allegedly*, he says.

Somebody barks.

Somebody yelps.

Somebody howls.

Nate says, "I have a neighbor who is harassing my dogs. The bitch. But it's not her *fault*, though, because ever since she had brain surgery she's been fucked up."

Bjarki says, "Nate's forcing this elderly, feeble-minded woman to court."

"She's a sixty-year-old, overweight, smoking widow."

I say something about a smoking widow.

Nate says she's the other kind of smoking widow.

Chapter 4-2.3 of the Farmington Town Code reads:

An owner who keeps or maintains a dog or dogs whose barking, howling, or yelping sustained for one hour or intermittently for three hours, can be heard at or beyond the boundary of the property on which the dog(s) is(are) located, violates this section, and has created a nuisance.

Nate isn't arguing the point of nuisance. But, he says—*but*—what is the definition of *intermittent*? What is the definition of *an hour straight*? Technically, his dogs have been barking intermittently since he got them like eight years ago. But on the other hand, technically, his dogs have never barked for an hour straight. And in addition, Nate says, there's an *exemption* in the code for rescue dogs, which one of *his* dogs *is*.

For a moment, we consider the concept of a rescue human, but not very seriously.

Nate says the rules are retarded. He hopes the judge isn't a cat person.

Nate says, "Did you get some good quotes of Hunter telling Menno what to do and Menno saying, 'What?'"

Hunter is a college student who, because of the virus, is on leave from college.

Out in the yard, Menno told me a couple jokes.

"Oh god! Which ones?"

"The bad one. He made me promise not to put it in The Book."

"Yeah, that'd be—yeah."

"Dude, are the Amish just super racist? Is that, like, their thing?" These are the exact words that I say. This is how I talk.

Nate says, "I think they're super *sheltered*."

Bjarki says, "He told a *racist* joke?"

"You already know it."

"I do?"

Nate tells the joke.

Bjarki says, "What's the *difference*?"

Nate says, "What's the difference."

"But if you think a certain way and it's not *based* on anything and you're like, 'I just feel that way,' then I'm gonna be like, 'Okay, but why?' 'Oh, because I just don't like Black people.' 'Okay, but why?' 'Because they all suck.' 'Okay, but do they?' 'Yeah. You've seen them. You know.' And it's like, 'Well, no, I *don't know*.' I've actually seen a lot of way suckier white people than black people."

Bjarki's worried that Menno, the young Amish man starting at The Wood Mill in a month, will insist on doing things a certain way, rather than The Wood Mill's way.

Nate says, "I don't think he's gonna do a good job."

Why?

"I just don't."

Bjarki says, "So are the Amish the ultimate brainwashed society, or—"

"—We are." A fly on the wall in here would never last a day.

"*We are!*"

"—Or are they the most liberated and free?"

"They can't use zippers."

"Why? *Why?*"

"Maybe he had snaps, or buttons. You've got to have something."

"How many kids did he have?"

"Eighteen."

"*Eighteen!*"

"Eighteen kids in twenty-two years."

"She's pretty much spitting one out every nine and a half months, like, *boom*. They probably just *fall* out. Your body's just like, 'Nope, we're going to stay dilated.'"

I say something about a clasp system. "To keep the baby in," I say.

"The Amish Incubation System 3000."

Nate, acknowledging the offense in our humor, says, "Oh it's so bad." Then he says, "You should make fun of everyone. We're all fucked-up."

Bjarki says, "I wonder what Amish people say about white people? Like normal white people. 'Get a load of this guy's forklift!' 'Look at this idiot. He hired an excavator for two hundred fifty bucks when I've got forty kids who can dig this trench for free!'"

Nate says, "People aren't going to be too mad about me, are they?"
    He's talking about you.
    I say, "They're going to love everybody."
    "They're going to love everybody!"

Bjarki says, "Nate, I got some bad news."
    Nate says, "What you got?"
    "Matthew's floor cupped."
    Nate says, "Who's Matthew?"

The shadow of an intruder darts past an elderly woman's window. It's nighttime, obviously. The woman calls 911 and gets a prerecorded response. *"If it's, like, a rape, press 1. If it's, like, a this, press 2.* And then it's like, *Estimated response time: six days. This is what it will be like if what's his face wins."*
    "Joe Biden," Bjarki says.
    "It's Trump humor, because obviously he threw the word *rape* in there."
    Bjarki says that Donald Trump *has* made references to Mexicans being rapists.
    Nate says Trump also said something about black dudes impregnating white girls.
    Bjarki says, "That was our governor."
    At a town hall in 2016, Paul LePage, Maine's two-term Republican governor, said, "These are guys with the name D-Money, Smoothie, Shifty—these types of guys. . . . They come up here. They sell their heroin. They go back home. Incidentally, half the time, they impregnate a young white girl before they leave, which is a real sad thing because then we have another issue we have to deal with."
    Nate says, "It's not like that's *that wrong*. It's stupid white fat chicks on drugs who have no money and so the black dudes fuck 'em and give them money."
    No one says anything.

Nate says, "Speaking of fucktards," and Bjarki says, "Uh-oh," and we both kind of wince in anticipation of whatever Nate is going to say next, which is that Tyler, the now-former Wood Mill employee of the Extension Cord Fiasco, was recently beaten up by a marine. Nate says the dude stomped Tyler's head because Tyler was dating the marine's fifteen-year-old sister.

Bjarki wants to see pictures.

Maybe something's gotten into me. I say it's not okay to beat people up.

"I don't know. Beating up someone who's having sex with a minor seems kind of justified."

"Say you have a fifteen-year-old sister and some twenty-year-old scuzzy kid is banging her. What would you do?"

I say, "I'm pretty sure I wouldn't stomp anyone's head." I don't even touch *scuzzy kid*. In that moment, I'm feeling more than slightly disoriented about right and wrong as it pertains to Tyler and the marine and the marine's younger sister, and also The World, where someone—a U.S. marine—might stomp you because, presumably, he thinks you've transgressed against him or his sister or whatever and then someone might recount the stomping with glee and someone else might want to see photos of the gore and someone else might listen to the retelling with rapt curiosity thinking it's great material for a book about floorboards, and yes, I know, transgression is complicated, and consent too, and justice, but once the stomping starts, I'm thinking— ignoring the previous centuries of stomping—who or what will save us from the stomping apocalypse?

Well, that's easy, at least in theory. That's why we have laws. And police. Except it gets a lot more complicated if you are a black man in Maine who the governor refers to as Smoothie. Or a black man in Minnesota named George Floyd. And what are the real rights of a fifteen-year-old girl? Or a U.S. marine? Or a fatherless twenty-year-old?

I knew Tyler had grown up without a dad because Ethan had called him a "mama's boy." I'd never heard someone say "mama's boy" without judgment, but that's how Ethan said it. He meant it in the sense that Tyler had been raised by a single mom and that he hadn't had a father to teach him fatherly things.

Nate said, "If you grow up in Maine, you've probably picked up a hammer."

Ethan said, "Tyler never did."

Nate said, "Reading a tape measure, Tyler'd be like, 'It's four little ticks.'"

Nate says, "What the *fuck* are you talking about, *ticks*?"

Tyler says, "*Wool*, the little lines."

"Those are sixteenths. Read it to me in sixteenths."

"Four sixteenths?"

"Yes. Great. Let's start there. All the little lines *mean* something."

So Nate had taught Tyler about tape measures, but who had taught Tyler about the rest of it? And how about Nate? Or you or me or the marine? Had America taught the marine? Hadn't we all learned how to behave—how to *be*—from some combination of someones somewhere, The World, I mean? And wasn't it less what The World had taught us and more how The World had *made us?*—which raised all kinds of questions about free will and justice and good and evil and probably also past life accumulations of karma, and it all makes me think about something I heard a Buddhist monk say near Mount Shasta a long time ago.

The monk turned to a boy in the crowd and, smiling, asked the boy's age.

The boy said he was eight.

The monk grinned at everything everyone said, I remember that.

Very good! he said, clapping. Whose fault is that?

We all squirmed a little.

Your fault! He shouted at the child's parents.

The parents grimaced.

The monk laughed. He pointed to the child. *Your* fault?

Your fault! He was pointing at all of us now.

We were searching our pockets, the ground, the sky.

The monk stuck his finger in his own chest, arching his brow. *My* fault?

He laughed and coughed and hacked and laughed.

He gazed toward the mountain.

Mountain fault?

World fault?

Everybody fault? *Nobody* fault?

Everybody fault! Nobody fault!

ELEVEN

Rangoon II (Eggplant)

"These logs are real," Travis Marble said significantly, but also softly, as if raising his voice might rouse and animate the slumbering tonnage of wood. How many tons of wood? A cubic foot of eastern white pine, on average— undried, wet, green—weighs about fifty-five pounds. The log was two feet across and sixteen and a half feet long, frozen through. The saw yard was just a patch of plowed ground beside a cemetery and an old weeviled pine. Broad flakes of snow fell around us—Travis, Bjarki, and me—lifted, floated, fell. This was March 2, 2020, a split second before the masks, the distancing, the shutdowns. We were 1,000 feet above sea level, thirty miles upstream from Bjarki's house, in the town of Avon, population 460, County Franklin. Across the frozen Sandy River, just over the hill—that's where Travis grew up. He'd begun sawing with his father in 1987, at the age of twelve, when he was *yay*

high. Now, standing in green boots, black pants, and a heavy green overshirt, he was grinning and stout, about twice as tall as *yay*. Last year, working with his wife, Elizabeth, and their sons, Travis sawed 350,000 board feet of boards, 63,000 of which belonged to The Wood Mill of Maine.

"The mill," Travis said, "just wants to eat." There was something familiar in his eyes, something gleefully prankster, shining and youthful that brought to mind a lobsterman I'd worked with during the past winter.

Pinkham had a bum hip and a shoulder tilted from a load carried too long. He called lobsters *bugs* or *critters*, said "beers" like *bee-uhs*, and referred to me as a honey badger. Honey badgers, Pinkham said, *didn't care*. We were working on a house overlooking an expanse of mudflats and often distracted ourselves by watching the men digging below.

Verming, Pinkham called it, the *V* almost silent, almost sounding like a *W*.

Blood- and sandworms can grow to be a foot long. Recreational fishermen use them for bait. In 2018, Maine worm diggers sold $7.5 million worth of worms. Vermers, Pinkham said, were notorious. On the hierarchy of those earning a living from the sea, they were near the bottom, below the urchin divers, the winklers, the clammers, the hoggers, the draggers, the shrimpers and—of course—the lobstermen.

Pinkham was what some people in Maine might have called *rough* and what some might have called *ignorant* and what some might have called a *redneck* or a *hick* or a *creature* or a *critter* or a *creeper* or a *clown* or an *islander* or a *buffalo* or a *pirate* or *a real Mainer*. (*Buffalo* has racist origins.) Sometimes we called Pinkham, Pink*man*, or *Pinky,* or *Stinkham*, and sometimes we complained that he smelled like bait (which wasn't true), but mostly I just called him by his first name, which was D. Since D was fourteen years old—yay high—he'd worked on fishing boats. He could coil an extension cord or an air hose with more alacrity than any of us carpenters. He read paperbacks in the shower. There were soda cans and bait trays in the bed of his truck, air fresheners hanging from the rearview, coins and candy wrappers on the dash, all of which he called *cultch*. In grade school, you would have called him a *motormouth*. He was not oblivious to his garrulousness. He said that while working alone on his lobster boat in the summer, he was saving up his words for use in the winter. For instance, one week, all I heard about was bald eagle sex—the way they copulated in free fall, first flying high together, then locking talons and plummeting, making bald eagle babies all the way down.

D—he has a precocious sense of melodrama. One day he turns to me and says, "I think I'd like to have bald eagle sex."

What could I say?

"Me too," says I.

In fact, the raptor's acrobatics are a ritual of courtship, not intercourse, but we didn't know that. D had four kids and he talked to his wife on the phone about six times a day, always telling her he loved her, about six times per call, and all of that, or, really, the sense of D—the sense of him standing beside me—was present as I stood beside Travis.

"Moose is fun," Travis said. It seemed he wanted to talk about anything but sawing, preferably hunting, specifically moose, which he could summon with a call that sounds a little like an abbreviated goose honk, or a frog, or a groaning floorboard. Chopped up and canned, one moose fills about eighty quart-size jars. That's a lot of breakfast. *Cronches*, Travis called the biggest bulls. He'd been lucky hunting recently, especially so since moose populations in the Northeast are being decimated by creatures a fraction of their size. Dead moose have been found hosting as many as one hundred thousand moose ticks (*Dermacentor albipictus*) (aka winter ticks), each capable of ingesting as much as four milliliters of blood. The math isn't great for the moose. Cows become less fertile. Fewer calves survive the winter. (Deer ticks, or *Ixodes scapularis*, which carry Lyme, anaplasmosis, babeseosis, and Powassan encephalitis, are also proliferating.) In spring, satiated moose ticks depart their hosts to lay as many as four thousand eggs in the forest duff. Whereas in previous decades they encountered the perils of snow and frost, now they find a consistently thawed and hospitable earth. (Since 1895, Maine's average annual air temperature has increased 3.2 degrees. Over the past century, winters in Maine have decreased in length by two weeks.) The six-legged larvae—*seed ticks*, they're called—hatch in May and survive through the summer on the nutrients from their mother. In early fall, mobs of the poppy seed–sized critters clamber up brush and trees. They gather at the tips of twigs and branches and interlock appendages—a thousandfold riot of ticks, all hoping to hitch a ride—*questing*, it's called.

For better or worse, we were all rooting against the tick.

But about them logs—*mostly* they'd been opening up good, some *real* good. One, however, was about the worst Travis had ever sawed for The Wood Mill. It was so bad he couldn't even salvage sheathing boards from it, let alone flooring. Thanks, Nate. The log was a pile of four-by-four bunks now, all of them honeycombed with red rot, the result of a fungal infection that can undermine the wood's strength. Bunks go beneath stacks of lumber. In the hierarchy of timber products, they're at the bottom, below shavings in a dead heat with sawdust.

Nearby, a pile of slabs was piled higher than the snowbanks. A *slab*, with one round barky-face and one flat-sawn face, is the first board cut from a log.

"It's a poor area," Travis said. "Guys come and take them slabs and the only thing I tell them is, 'If you can use it, *you* use it, because if *you* can't, there's somebody else who can.'"

Sawdust was for the cows.

Travis's Wood-Mizer LT50 portable sawmill is an orange insectoid-looking thing. The engine and the gas tank and the saw head crouch above the long log bed. The blade is a hoop of toothed metal. The log before us, with its two square sides, could now fairly be called a *cant*.

Did Travis want to saw a couple of boards so I could watch?

"Not really."

He said, "Where are you from?"

He said, "Tell me what you're doing anyway."

Sawing boards from the top of the cant to the bottom, as all of The Wood Mill's flooring is sawn, is called *plain* or *flat* sawing. Look at the end of a board. The curve and orientation of the annual growth rings will tell you from where in the log the board came. In the designations of lumbering, growth rings oriented to the board's face from 0 to 45 degrees—arching across the end of the board like the bands of a rainbow—designate flat-sawn lumber. However, as the sawyer saws, this pattern will change. The board cut from the very center of the cant will resemble a board that has been *quarter sawn*. (In quarter-sawn boards, the growth rings are oriented at nearly 90 degrees to the face of the board. Some people call these boards vertical-grain boards, but VG is a bit of a misnomer, referring as it does to growth rings, not grain.)

(Quarter-sawn boards are valued because of their straightness and stability.) And because each flat-sawn board comes from a unique latitude in a cant, the patterns on each board's face, the board's *figure*—what is commonly called grain but is not technically grain—will vary dramatically from one board to the next, from one side of the log to the other. (*Grain* refers to the orientation of wood cells (tracheids in conifers) and can be, among other things, *tight, straight, sweepy, spirally, curly, cross, knotty*.) A good way to see what I'm talking about is to draw several concentric circles. Each circle—the penciled ring *and* the white space—represents one year's worth of woody growth. The space between each of the penciled rings represents *earlywood*, or *springwood*, or *newwood*, the faster growing, less dense wood produced (in Maine) from spring to early summer. The penciled rings represent wood grown at the end of the season, the denser *latewood*. (Drill through multiple growth rings. You'll feel each one.)

But what is wood?

In some very literal ways, wood is produced from thin air, though textbook biology (which is, to an extent, literally true) asserts that wood originates from a single layer of cells located below the tree's bark. This is the cambium layer, which, technically, is not wood. (Technically, your mother is not you, but it is from her that you are born.) (Technically, the book is not the author, but . . .) Wood is created *within* the cambium layer's ever-expanding circumference. This causes the branches and the roots and the trunk of the tree to thicken (a process called *secondary growth*), though not necessarily constantly or uniformly throughout the tree. (At the same time, the tree might also be growing upward in distinctly different processes (*primary growth*).) Once a ring of growth (a growth ring) (xylem) (wood) forms, this ring (for our purposes) does not grow or shrink but rather becomes encased in the next ring of growth (wood). (A ring isn't necessarily a circle.) (In some parts of the world, where the growing season varies less dramatically, annual growth rings may not appear in a log at all or, depending on rain or drought or insects, there may be many discernible rings in a single year.) (In dendrochronology, tree rings are studied for information about the past: climatic variations, pest invasions, fires.) (It is said that some Native people of the northeast occasionally consumed the inner bark (phloem) and cambium layer of eastern white pine trees, which contain dietary fiber, carbohydrates, vitamin C, and minerals. (Porcupines love phloem.) (Girdling a tree involves cutting through the cambium layer around a tree's entire circumference. The tree will die above the girdle.) (The Native (Indigenous) (American (Indian)) people (who did not refer to themselves as the Native (Indigenous) (American (Indian)) people) of the Northeast have sometimes been referred to as *barkeaters*.) (Wabanaki generally refers to the people who have lived since the glaciers receded in The Dawnland, or, The Place of the Dawn. There may once have been as many as twenty tribes residing here: Maliseet, Mi'kmaq, Passamaquoddy, Penobscot (to name a few (while also acknowledging that the spelling (in English) isn't totally agreed upon))).) (By the time the Pilgrims (who did not refer to themselves as the Pilgrims) arrived in Plymouth (which was not yet known as Plymouth), between 75 and 90 percent of the Native people in the Northeast had been killed by disease, most likely caused by a virus brought to North America by Europeans.) (On December 16, the *Mayflower*, carrying 101 people, arrives at what will become Plymouth Harbor. On shore, there are

> great Oakes but not very thicke, Pines, Wal-nuts, Beech, Ash, Birch, Hasell, Holley, Asp, Sasifras, in abundance, & Vines everywhere, Cherry trees, Plum-trees . . . there is a greate deale of Land cleared, and hath beene planted with Corne three or four yeares agoe . . . our greatest labour will be fetching of our wood.

The town is plotted in two rows. Without horses or oxen or mules, the settlers transport timber and firewood by handcart and sled. They build clumsy house frames covered with wattle and daub (a mixture of clay, straw, twigs, leaves). Roofs are thatched. Chimneys are made from clay-lined timbers. Roofs burn. A rainstorm dissolves the walls of houses. The winter is mercifully mild and yet, by spring, half of the Pilgrims are dead.

On March 16, Samoset, a man from Pemaquid, arrives.

> He saluted us in English . . . he was a tall straight man, the haire of his head blacke, long behind, only short before, none on his face at all; he

asked some beere, but we gave him strong water, a bisket, and butter, and cheese, & pudding, and a peece of a mallerd, all which he liked well . . . he told us the place where we now live, is called, Patuxet and that about foure yeares agoe, all the Inhabitants dyed of an extraordinary plague, and there is neither man, woman, nor childe remaining.)

(Some observers likened this disease to the Black Plague, but in reality, mortality rates were twice as high in North America as they had been in fourteenth-century Europe.) (There is no annual growth ring equivalent in the human body.) (Your age is hearsay.) (How often have the world's Indigenous peoples been confined to history's parenthesis?) (Have you ever been confined to a parenthesis?) (When we say a virus can *survive* on a surface or in the air, we don't mean that it can *live*.)

But *what* is wood?

Functionally, in a tree, wood delivers water to the leaves from the roots and disburses the sugars produced by the leaves in photosynthesis—the photosynthate. All plants have systems to perform this transport function, but what makes wood special is its combination of lightness, rigidity, and flexibility, which allows trees to grow taller than any other life on Earth. (The tallest, a redwood, *Sequoia sempervirens,* is 380 feet tall.) (*Pinus strobus* is the tallest tree in the northeast, reaching 200 feet.) (It's not the size that matters.) Grasses, though they may seem woody, do not contain wood. Neither does a palm tree contain wood. In fact, a palm tree, like a banana tree, is not (by some definitions) even a tree. *Tree* is not a taxonomical group. (There may be as many as three trillion "trees" living on Earth.) A cork tree is made of wood, though cork itself is not. Cork is bark. Neither do leaves nor needles contain wood, though twigs do. And roots too. And shrubs and bushes. And the bench I made for B, and the bed and the box and the table and the desk. Carpenter ants live in wood. However, contrary to common belief, they do not eat it. They excavate. Rot is decay, a vernacular expression for decomposition. (Fungi (neither plant nor animal) play an integral role in the recycling of nutrients in forest ecosystems, turning fallen trees and plant matter into rich fertile humus. (Only fungi (and some bacteria) can break down lignin, the compound that lends strength and rigidity to wood-cell walls.)

In addition, dense branching networks of mycorrhizae (literally, "fungus-root") in the soil connect the root systems of trees, even across species, allowing them to share sugars and send chemical "messages" about drought, blight, nutrient shortages, and surpluses.) (The biggest oldest trees (mother trees) are connected to the most extensive mycorrhizae networks.) (Some forest ecologists speak of the collective "wisdom" of a forest.) (The bicolored deceiver fungus (*Laccaria bicolor*) produces a small mushroom often found in coniferous forests. Soil ecologists have tracked the movement of nitrogen from the bodies of tiny snow fleas to *Pinus strobus* seedlings. Between the fleas and the trees was the *Laccaria*, which had digested the bugs and fed them to the pines. In fact, 25 percent of all the nitrogen in the seedlings could be traced back to the snow fleas.) Red rot, heart rot, needle drop, blister rust.

But what is *wood*?

Consider the teenager's nomenclature for an erect pecker. A peckerwood is a jerk. A woodpecker is a bird. A group of woodcocks is a fall. A flock of seagulls is annoying. Though wooden rafters support your roof, there is no wood in a rafter of turkeys. There are wood ducks, woodchucks, Wood Islands, Woodvilles, Wood Alleys, none of them as wooden as the personalities of your dead neighbors, Mr. and Mrs. Wood, who are both just as stiff as a board, lying, as they are, god bless them, in their old pine boxes. I would, you would, she would: it's conditional. Wings of ash and spruce flew the Wright brothers a few yards. Blasted into space, a piece of Newton's apple tree achieved weightlessness. Forests, you might say, are restless. Now, as the climate rapidly changes, they must move with it. Can they do this? Do they care? The willow weeps. Longfellow heard the pines *murmuring* and Thoreau heard them *soughing* and in them Whitman heard *liquid*. It's the pitch and the moisture in pine that pops when it burns. A cord of white pine contains 14,300 BTUs, roughly half the BTUs contained in red oak. A British thermal unit describes heat. Heat is energy. One British thermal unit is equivalent to 1,055 joules and will raise the temperature of 1 pound of water 1 degree Fahrenheit. (Joule was a person, James Prescott Joule, b. 1818, d. 1889.) A small diamond fell from your wedding ring and was never seen again. We searched beside the sink and the toilet and the tub. We tossed the sheets. Was that it glinting in a gap between our bedroom floorboards? It was sand. *To pine* is to yearn or to languish or to moon. To some lumbermen, a log is a *stick*. To a carpenter, a stick is a two-by-four. Stick it in the wall and it becomes a *stud*. To biologists, wood is heterogeneous, hygroscopic, cellular, and anisotropic. To materials scientists, it is orthotropic—just because a board may break as a bridge doesn't mean it will budge as a tower. In Latin it's *lignum*. In Greek, *xylon*. *Go, bois, khashab, madeira, mokuzai, mu*. Fuel, shelter, evil, sacred, junk. As you drive seventy-five miles per hour into the Pine Tree State, note the forked trunks of the weeviled pines. (The adult white pine weevil (*Pissodes strobi*) is about five millimeters long. Small antennae protrude from its snout-like beak. It prefers the vigorous leaders of young trees growing in full sun, which means that pines colonizing former fields are most susceptible to the weevil. A female lays eggs in cavities that she has excavated in the terminal shoot. When the larvae hatch, they form a "feeding ring" in and below the bark, effectively girdling the tree. The terminal shoot wilts, drooping like the crook in a shepherd's staff. (Some trees will successfully drown the weevils in sap.) After a pine loses its terminal shoot, lateral shoots will compete to be the new leader, creating a fork-trunked tree. (The Wood Mill of Maine does not want forked-trunk trees.) (And what do you want?)) (It was an unseasonably cold night, the night before we visited Travis. Bjarki had just asked me a question about The Book and I, as usual, it seemed, was struggling to articulate an answer that would suggest I knew exactly what I was doing, which of course I did not. We were at Thai Smile, a small flame between us.

I said, Imagine an eggplant. I said, I love how purple its skin is, its shine and its shape, how surprisingly lightweight it is. My sister grows them in her garden. My father is crazy for them, and I respect that, I do, how fanatical some eggplant lovers are, but, I said, you see, I am just not an Eggplant Man.

Bjarki, it turned out, felt a similar ambivalence toward zucchini.

As did I.

Connection via a squash was no small thing.

The point is, I said, a Pineapple Guy cannot just become an Eggplant Man. And I'm not saying I'm any kind of Pineapple Guy or anything, but even if I am, or was—or if you are, or were—that doesn't mean you can just transform an eggplant into a pineapple. Or vice versa. I mean, you can, but you also cannot. Do you see the difficulty here? I have, I said, been attempting to deny the existence of something that very clearly exists, to assert the existence of something that very clearly does not exist. (Eggplants were domesticated in South and East Asia more than two thousand years ago. The English called them *love apples* or *madde apples* or *raging apples*. "This plant groweth in Egypt," writes "John Gerarde of London" in 1597,

> bringing foorth fruite of the bigness of a great Cucumber . . . But I rath-er wishe Englishmen to content themselves with the meate and sauce of our owne countrey, then with fruite and sauce eaten with such perill: for doubtlesse these apples have a mischeevous qualitie.)

(Hence *madde* apples.) ("Fruits" "discovered" by Europeans were commonly referred to as *apples*.) (Pineapples were once known as *ananas*, though in 1624 Captain John Smith called the fruit *pineapple*, probably because it resembled a pine cone.) (In fact, the cones of pine trees were once called pine *apples*.) The wonton soup was like nothing I had ever tasted. This awareness arose in me, it seemed, nondualistically, and with it came the feeling that I was imitating something. A book maybe. But, I said, what I want to make clear is that I am *not* saying that I do or do not like eggplants. It's just that now (some of the time) I can accept the diversity of my feelings for them. In fact, I'll admit, I like their decorative potential. Metaphorically and phonetically, they're stupendous. Baba ghanoush, ratatouille, etc., etc.

And Bjarki—god bless him—he was nodding along like he had no idea what I was talking about.

He said, How long is The Book going to be?

I swear, Tourette's appeals to me. It has its own perfections. I love chop-sticks and Tootsie Rolls and dragonflies. I love sunshine and whiskey and the way blue sky leaks into a daytime moon, flooding its craters so that the satellite appears transparent. I love purple too and smelling and your enjoy-ing face. I have never been as cool as I wanted to be. It was just the kindness in his question, and his curiosity, and his pride, I suppose, this sense that he was excited to be a part of The Book and that he was hoping The Book would be a big book because bigness, as all of us Americans know, is akin to goodness, and if I were to write a Big Book about Bjarki, then this, by our American logic, would suggest that Bjarki was good, which—believing that you are good—I have always thought of as a good thing (as long as you aren't harming anyone (though what is *harming*?)) and so his question made *me* feel good too.

Or, to put it more simply, it was just *him*.

And at the same time, I knew that it was blasphemous. (And also magnificent.) (Also cliché.) Imagine if you loved everyone bruising produce at the grocery. They'd lock you up. But then again, tell me I'm being hyperbolic when I say the shit hit the fan long ago. In fact, I think that we love each other without saying it or knowing it all the time—or without *allowing* ourselves to know it. (My family, for instance—the Puritan runs strong among us—has never said those three words easily. (You could say we say I love you between the lines.) (This I recount with wonder and rangoon, without bitterness.) (But did the Puritans not love?)) (You will know a pineapple is ripe by the color and the smell.) (Pine trees, I believe, are contagious.) (The apples of *Pinus strobus* are four to eight inches long and mature in two years. They are clustered, pendent, symmetric, cylindric. The scales open in the late summer of their second season, releasing seeds, about two per scale.) (One ninety-year-old stand of white pine was found to produce about sixty-five pounds of seeds per acre, 26,500 seeds per pound.) (Squirrels do beautiful things to pinecones, scattering the scales like petals.) (I don't mean to dissemble.) (I'm not saying I know what you feel.) (Loving isn't always pure or simple.) (You and I do very unlovely things.) (Take, for example, an account of George Waymouth's 1604 journey up the Maine coast, describing a magnetized sword:

> Our Captaine showed [the Native people] a strange thing which they soondred at. His sword and mine having beene touched with the Loadstone, took up a knife, and held it fast . . . whereat they much marvelled. This we did to cause them to imagine some great power in us: and for that to love and feare us.)

I said an unfathomable length, an incomprehensible number of pages.

The waiter said, "I think shrimp inside."

Bjarki said, "I think that's tuna."

Why no one said eel is beyond me. He offered me a bite. In the rings of Bjarki's Dragon Roll, I was certain only generally of the taste and the texture and the colors and the rice.) (Rice and pasta and red pasta sauce and white pasta sauce and granola bars and Nutella filled Bjarki's pantry—three hundred dollars' worth, he said. He wasn't worried about the virus, but rather shortages, inflations, riots. We'd just returned from Thai Smile and as we talked about the stockpiling of toilet paper and the politics of naming the virus, I drank another beer and then another and then I started burping loudly whenever Bjarki said something objectionable—objectionable *to me*, that is—like when he implied that climate change was a hoax because, he said, first it was called global *warming* and now it was called global *climate change* and this *rebranding*, he said, to suit the hoaxers' narrative (a very literary word, *narrative*) undermined all the supposed science of the whole thing, the whole thing being the vibration of certain molecular bonds in the atmosphere. Plus, had I noticed that real estate was a hot commodity in Florida? Investors wouldn't be buying down there if *the whole state* was underwater ten years *ago*, as predicted in that movie, *An Inconvenient Truth*.

"Which you haven't even watched," I said.

"Actually," he said, "I did watch it."

On September 2, 2019, Bjarki's exact words to me, as they are digitally preserved on my Voice Memos app, were "I've never seen it."

"So you *did* watch it?" I was sitting on the couch in the living room.

"*An Inconvenient Truth*? Yes." He was sitting on a stool in the kitchen.

The kitchen and the living room are basically one room. We were in the same room in the same house is what I'm saying.

M: So you *did*? I thought you said that you *didn't*.

B: I saw the first one in high school. Even then I realized it was dumb.

What was said next I barely heard. ("Maybe now we're like ten thousand miles closer to the sun. Can we measure that? And the fucking magnetic poles—they switch every twenty-five thousand years. All kinds of weird shit goes on.") ("Remember the supposed hole in the ozone layer? Whatever happened to that?") ("These nickel mines are about the worst thing that's ever happened to humanity.") The fact that Bjarki seemed to be okay with sometimes lying to me must, I felt, mean something big and destructive about our connection or our lack of connection. Or maybe it meant nothing, because humans lie all the time and hadn't I told a million lies in my life, to myself and to others, and didn't our president lie unabashedly? Still, betrayal is never not unlovely. The World must conform to my understanding of The World, and to that end, I can be as righteous as anybody. (On the Massachusetts Bay Colony seal, created in 1629, leaves conceal a man's waist. Behind him are two towering pines. In one hand, the man holds a bow and in the other, an arrow. A ribbon of speech flies from his mouth, COME OVER AND HELP US. It is a cunning piece of propaganda, suggesting, as it does, that the Native people *want* to be saved. As disease ravages the Northeast, only the pale, bearded men, in their loud boots and funny jackets, seem to go unharmed, and many Native people, in desperation, or out of some clairvoyance, or because of the cunning of missionaries, convert to Christianity.

Towns are established to corral and convert at Natick, Namasket, Punkapog, Nashoba, Wamesit, Hassanamesit. In 1661, fifteen hundred copies of the New Testament are published in the Wampanoag language. Though some Native people learn English, the English generally refuse to learn any Native languages. (The legacy of forced adoption and forced acculturation (conversion) will be repeated for the next four hundred years.)

The "poore Indians" live in "hellish darknesse," reports *New England's First Fruits*, a Harvard publication, in 1643, "adoring the Divell himselfe for their GOD."

Some Europeans believe that the very land corrupts. "What should bee the reason of this mighty difference," Roger Williams, a Quaker, wonders,

> that all the Sonnes of men on this side the way should have such plenteous clothing for Body, for Soule! and the rest of Adam's sonnes and Daughters on the other side, or in America, should neither have nor desire clothing for their naked soules, or Bodies?

John Josselyn describes the Native people like trees, as "tall and handsome timber'd," and on colonial maps, trees indicate the habitations of Indians while steeples indicate the habitations of the English. "They say themselves," Williams reports, "that they have sprung and grown up in that very place, like the very trees of the Wildernesse." The Native people and trees and sin are conflated. The English fear losing their Englishness—their identity, their purity—to this corrupt land. Axes are sharpened, fields plowed, rifles polished, alcohol poured.

In 1651, some Norridgewock people tell French missionaries that "the Demon of drunkenness . . . causes murders among us and makes us like madmen."

The Jesuits report,

All the Allied Savages dwelling on the Kennebec hate firewater as much as they hate the Iroquois; and if [the English] have any more of it brought hither to sell to the Savages, the latter will believe the English wish to exterminate them.

In fact, the language of extermination is often cloaked in the rhetoric of progress, righteousness, and divine ordination. For example, in his 1637 "Description of the Indians of New England," Thomas Morton writes,

The hand of God fell heavily upon them, with such a mortal stroke that they died on heaps as they lay in their houses; and the living, that were able to shift for themselves, would run away and let them die, and let their carcasses lie above the ground without burial. For in a place where many inhabited, there hath been but one left alive to tell what became of the rest; . . . the dead, they were left for Crows, Kites and vermin to pray upon. And the bones and skulls . . . made such a spectacle after my coming into those parts, that, as I traveled in that Forrest near the Massachusetts, it seemed to me a new found Golgatha. . . . And the place is made so much the more fit for the English Nation to inhabit in, and erect in it Temples to the glory of God.

Other times, extermination is explicit. In 1675, the Massachusetts Bay Colony decrees that

> it shall be lawful for any person, whether English or Indian, that shall find any Indian traveling or skulking in any of our Towns or Woods . . . to command them under their Guard and Examination, or to kill and destroy them as they best may or can.

Oh! It was grotesque, the way I gave it to Bjarki on the couch, shouting about floods and droughts and disease, the spit and the sweat flying. All I saw was aubergine. A heart attack took my father's father. My mother's father was a preacher. B had moved out the month before. Bjarki, on his stool in the kitchen, was grinning, the little devil, like he was enjoying the whole thing. I got up and walked to the sliding door. There was the quick fog of my breath on the glass and then the bright quarter of the moon beyond and above. But, I thought, was I actually seeing the moon, or only the sun's light reflecting off the moon, bent by gravity and then refracted through the atmosphere and then refracted again through the sliding glass and then again through the fog of my breath and then again through the lens of my eye before being absorbed by the photoreceptor cells on my retina (rods and cones), which then sent an electrical impulse through my optic nerve to my visual cortex and . . . . What did it even mean to *see*? I stepped outside. I love woods at night, in winter—leafless, open—lit as if from below. It's not any big revelation or anything but you can see into them. Even if I was able to muster some incredibly cunning argument, I would never disprove anything Bjarki had said—not to his satisfaction anyway. All I could do was cite my own life (more ticks, less snow) and whatever popular media I had read (I had read nothing about nickel mines) and the supposed scientific consensus, except that there was no way to *prove* that consensus, not without surveying every scientist with Bjarki along as witness. But what was most troubling, I thought, walking back to the house, was that Bjarki thought what I had said was empirically false and I thought what he had said was empirically false and at some level both of us were right. But then from another perspective, a more important perspective, I felt, he was way more wrong than I was, which is exactly what he would say about what *I* was saying, except, I felt, in that case, *he'd* be wrong.

(An eggplant is classified like a banana, as a "berry.")

(A berry is a "fleshy" "fruit" without a "stone.")

(Define *fleshy*, define *fruit*, define *stone*.)

(Define *define*.)

(A fungus is not a fruit, but a mushroom is the fruit of a fungus.)

(In 1623, the Wampanoag sachem Conbitant said to the English, "If your love is so great and it grows such good fruits, why is it that when you come to our places or we go to yours, you stand as if ready to fight, with the mouths of your guns pointed at us?")

("I saw the English took much ground, and I thought if I prayed, the English would not take away my ground.")

(Is *learning* different from *converting to new knowledge*? Different from *being* converted?)

(If you convert, you will become a better (superior) person.)

(Therefore, if you convert, The World will become a better (superior) place.)

(Do I want to convert The World?)

(There is only conversion—change—a contradiction in terms.)

(Is not the urge to fitness, to power, to superiority, written in our genes?)

(Whose fault?)

(Can Roger Williams really not *see* the clothes the Native people wear?)

(When deities first occupied the sky, the forest canopy was an unwelcome separation.)

(*Pinus strobus*, a pioneer species, will colonize former agricultural land so thickly its shade prevents the growth of future generations of pine.)

(Winter ticks are understood to be native to Maine.)

(It is easy to see *how* or *why* some people *believe* themselves superior.)

(Of course, I believe that I am superior to a white supremacist, and a murderer and any wrongdoer.)

(Of course, I know that I am not.)

(So, do I want to be *inferior*?)

(Is the most inferior actually the most *superior*, meaning it isn't *inferior* at all?)

(You must decide which wolf to feed.)

(During King Philip's War, the Native people had, according to Roger Williams, "forgot they were Mankind, and ran about the Countrie like Wolves tearing and Devouring the Innocent.")

("Savages," "Natives," "Barbarians," "Cannibals," "Heathens," "Devils," "Indians," etc.)

(Can that which necessarily objectifies—language—actually *humanize*?)

(Henry David Thoreau wrote that nothing stands up more free from blame than a pine tree.) (Go fuck yourself, Henry, with your cabin and your wisdom and your immortality.) (I love you. I love you. I love you.) In the morning, before we drive to visit Travis, there are red coals visible through the smudged glass of the stove and the sun isn't quite up and I fold the star-covered blanket on the couch and I hear Bjarki hit snooze in his room and out the window I see a dozen turkeys crossing the field that has been dusted with snow and I hear Bjarki hitting snooze again and on the counter I see a note from his mother, who has recently visited, listing the brownies and whipped cream and meals she prepared for him, and then the snooze again, and minutes later in the 10-degree cold the visible exhaust from the Sequoia, and our visible breath, mingling, or not, and then steaming cups of coffee at Christy's and behind us in line a man wrangling in his arms like unruly infants a bag of Cheetos and a bottle of wine.

As we drive west, we pass a commercial row called the Eastside Mall. Bjarki looks at me, grinning, rapping, all traces of whatever we felt last night gone. *"Just hit the East Side of the L-B-C on a mission tryin' to find Mister Matthew C."*

And I'm nodding my head like *Yeah! Yeah!*

"That's Nate Dogg," Bjarki says.

"Warren G," I insist, erroneously as it turns out.

Travis starts the Wood-Mizer. The orange sawhead descends, lowering the blade to an elevation an inch and five-thirty-seconds below the top of the cant. The moving blade cuts easily into the log, emitting a whining hum— *whimming*. Sawdust shoots to the side.

Elizabeth is standing at the end of the mill bed, waiting. She wears blue jeans tucked into knee-high green boots, a puffy red vest, no hat. Her brown hair falls past shoulders hunched against the cold. She steps forward to retrieve the board. She pulls, then pulls harder. She pushes. She shoves. Unbeknownst to us, behind the sawing blade, the board has refrozen to the cant. What was once one, and then two, has become one again. Travis walks to the other side of the cant, opposite Elizabeth. They push, pull, pry, curse, thump, finally working the board loose with a metal bar. When there are three stacks of ten freshly sawn boards, Travis slides the tines of a forklift into the space beneath the stacks—the space created by the bunks. He pivots, boards flapping.

Of all the wood Travis saws, he likes sawing pine best, despite its significant heft. "Pick up one of them small fuckers," he says, pointing to a slab. I look at Elizabeth. "You do that all day—that right there is hard on the body. We *work*, but I *like* to play. Our most favorite thing is, she'll drive me around and I'll drink beer. You know? We like to ride back roads."

Elizabeth shakes her head.

"You know it's true."

"I don't know that."

"But as far as sawing," Travis says, "I love pine."

Why does Travis love pine?

The smell.

And what does pine smell like?

Pine smells like pine.

TWELVE

Blue Stain

The boards arrive in winter, on flatbed eighteen-wheelers that sit idling in the chord of diesel as the packs are disembarked by forklift. A pack of pine—four feet wide, four feet tall, and sixteen feet long—contains between twelve hundred and fifteen hundred square feet of future floor. There are twelve packs on a truck. The boards are heavy with water, with ice. They are rough to the touch, each marked by the saw that cut it from the log. Travis Marble's band saw leaves regular grooves perpendicular to the length of the board. The Piete brothers, in Vermont, from whom Bjarki will sometimes buy a load, use a circular saw. Put your gloves on. It's time to pick those packs apart. Board by board, each solid pack is disassembled and then reassembled into a stickered pack. A sticker is a stick—one inch by one and a half inches by four feet, ideally made from hemlock or oak or ash or plywood. Between each layer of boards, they are placed crosswise, at regular intervals, facilitating an evaporative flow of air.

Why aren't pine stickers used to sticker a pack of pine?

"Green white pine on green white pine? The blue stain will creep in."

By *green*, Nate does not mean the color green. He means unseasoned, undried, wet.

By *blue*, however, he does mean the color blue, and also fifty different shades of gray, or even occasionally yellow, orange, purple, green, or red. Ghostly streaks wash through otherwise clean, rot-free wood, suggesting the work of an avant-garde watercolorist or, perhaps, a drunk. The artist, in this case, is microscopic, a fungi that feasts on the sugars, proteins, starches, and fats stored in phloem and sapwood, synthesizing melanin, a natural pigment that colors human hair and skin, the irises of your eyes. In fact, some people swoon for blue stain. *Denim pine*, they call it, paying through the nose. To them, it has character, charisma, drama. At The Wood Mill, however, where a board's value depends on purity, blue stain is bad news.

Blue stains prefer temperatures above 35 degrees. They thrive in wet wood—though not *too* wet, which is why some mills store boards under continuously sprinkling sprinklers. Other mills treat the ends of boards with wax. Some use fungicides.

Today, imagine young Ethan Brown on the old Lull, presenting a stickered pack of pine to the kiln. The Lull isn't like those forks scooting around the aisles of Home Depot, not like Travis's fork. The Lull is long. With its telescoping boom, it is properly called a telehandler. This one is spackled with rust and tilts hard to the left, not because it's supposed to, but because, someone says, "It's fucked."

"I'm gonna fucking kill him," Nate says in the office one day. "I get that he's a kid, and that he's lost his way, but he's too fucking stupid. And Beej, you've helped him way more than you should. And I've tried to give him advice and Bob's talked to him, but nothing helps and I'm fucking done. There's a quote—I think it's Mark Twain, '*Never*'—aw fuck—'Never battle wits with stupid people'? Something like that. Meaning, you can't wrap your mind around what they're talking about."

"Ethan will, one day, be a grown-up."

"Or he'll be like his dad and he won't be! 'Hey, I've got a hangnail. I can't come in today!'"

"He has a *what*?"

"No. I was giving an example, like, 'I have a hangnail.'"

"I don't know, Nate," Bjarki says. "What were you doing at Ethan's age? Were you drinking? Partying? Driving drunk?"

"Ohfuckyeah. But I still showed up. Still worked my day."

Ethan started at The Wood Mill at the age of fifteen, bagging shavings for a dollar a bag. He was at that time living with his girlfriend, who was seventeen. Parents were somewhere—not there. Eventually, he was able to fill, on average, twenty-three bags of shavings in an hour. Now, on the fork, everyone agrees, he is tidy and gentle and fast.

"Ethan always says stuff about family and I'm like, 'Love your family all you want, but you don't have to like 'em.' His dad's a piece of shit. He's fifty years old and he still goes to jail, gets probation, gets fired for stealing shit. Pocketing bubble gum when you're fourteen—yeah, everyone does that. But stealing shit when you're a *grown-ass man*? *With kids*?"

On the office floor, a basket is filled with fresh corn on the cob. A gift from Turkey Tom. Bob, a recent hire working his last years before retirement, peels back a husk, notes pale, undeveloped kernels. "I said to Ethan, 'If I was Beej, I would have told you to sit your ass home and think about why I should still have you employed here on Monday.' I said, 'You're a good worker, but you got no education. You can't go to New Balance or Backyard Farms. Places like that won't hire you. You don't know how lucky you got it here, bud.'"

Bjarki agonized over Ethan. He talked about him with me, with his dad, with Myke, with, it seemed, even the windshield of the truck. Over a span of years, a raucous chorus of voices—all Bjarki's, varying in pitch and strain and conviction—conveyed as much about Bjarki (and a single person's multiplicity) as they did about Ethan.

"He was in a fight with his dad and he smashed up his dad's car with a baseball bat. Then he blamed someone else. A couple weeks ago, he said he was late because he had a flat tire, but that was a lie too."

"I don't know if he's ashamed, but I can tell you that his life is incredibly fucked. I probably only know 10 percent of what's going on."

"He works hard. As long as you give him tasks, he'll knock that to-do list out."

"He's never worked a forty-hour week."

"He's been to jail five or six times. Overnights, weekenders. A week here. I have no idea how many times."

"He's showing all the signs of being a drug addict, is what it is."

"He wasn't at the *dentist*. He's dealing with stuff at home and is too proud to say."

"*Josh* would have fired Ethan *years* ago."

"My employees are fed up because he's not pulling his weight."

"The first time I fired him was when the owner of Christy's told me he was smoking weed in their parking lot at lunchtime."

"I think about when I was nineteen. . . . Yeah, I drank. Yeah, I partied, but—"

"Ethan's a fucking broken human being."

"He has a *victim* mentality. He'll tell me ten reasons why everybody *else* forced him down this path."

"He can unload trucks quickly. He knows how to run the kilns. It's just that for every few days of good work, he makes a mistake that costs me hundreds if not thousands of dollars."

"I'm not trying to be a *big brother*. I feel *bad* for him."

"I think Ethan's here to stay now. I think he's realized he's got it pretty good and that I put up with a lot of shit."

"His dad's a fucking thief. He slashes people's tires and gets in bar fights. He's nothing but trouble everywhere he goes and everybody knows it."

"His paycheck goes to his parents. He's taking care of that household."

"Ethan could be letting things go. 'Oh, it fell in my pocket.' Sticky fingers kind of thing. We've had quite a bit go missing. I purchased ten batteries and numbered them one through ten. Where the fuck are batteries seven and eight?"

"Honestly, if this were a reality show, you wouldn't even need to create drama. *The Life of Ethan*: holy shit."

"The right thing to do is to shit can his ass. But . . . *fuckin'*. . . I can't. I *can't*, man. I've seen his whole life. You can't just throw these people out."

"Now what's unemployment? Who pays into that? We all do. And I know that when I fire him, he's going to fight me tooth and nail to collect it. That bothers me, like I've let the taxpayer down. I get that there needs to be some kind of failsafe, but my thinking is, when somebody gets real hungry, they're going to get their shit together."

"Honestly, the best thing that Ethan could do is join the military."

Bjarki sighs.

"When you interview him, I don't think you'll get anything of *quality* out of him."

I mean, it's possible that I'll meet with Ethan and afterward not have anything to write about, but, I'm thinking, how many times have I thought that what Bjarki was saying was without quality—whatever that means—and then, upon reflection, that material (*especially* that material) is what seems to be the *highest* quality and so I'm like, "He can't just be this presence in The Book that I never talk with and that you guys always bullshit about."

"It's not bullshit," Nate says. "It's factual. You want *his* perspective? That'd be a book in itself: *Ethan's Abstract View on Reality*."

"I mean, I hope he's honest, but I don't think he will be. And you won't know the difference."

There are so many people in the world that you will never know. And then the people that you actually do know—one study suggests that Americans "know" between ten and twenty-five people "well enough to trust"—they are basically a statistically insignificant quantity of people, at least in relation to the nearly eight billion people on the planet, a blip not even worth counting, basically nothing, nobody. *You* and *I* are basically nobody, is what I'm saying. But what really interests me is that we *think* we know everyone else on the planet, not carnally, but *enough* to despise them or laugh at them or dismiss them or maybe even love them—whatever *love* is—and we think that what we think we know about these people is the truth, or really we don't even stop to consider whether it is or isn't the truth at all, but instead just behave and feel accordingly. It's crazy, especially because *we do know* that what we think we know *isn't* the truth—certainly not the whole truth—if only because the truth is messy, elusive, and perhaps inarticulatable (not a word), and yet here we all are, strongly feeling things about the Vermers or the Massholes or whomever. Ourselves, even. Or, to put it more precisely, I haven't yet introduced myself to Ethan because I'm nervous about it, nervous that I am going to overcompensate for all those unconscious biases I'm sure I've developed from everything I've heard and that I'll end up being patronizingly nice and then, I'm also sure, Ethan will end up hating me. And I rather desperately want him to like me. If he likes me, then that will mean that whatever divides exist between us don't matter as much as they sometimes feel like they matter and it will mean that I am not a condescending elitist who thinks I'm better than him (or anyone) (which I don't), which I understand is a whole lot of my own personal bullshit that isn't fair to put on Ethan anyway.

Ethan steps into the office. He's wiry and pale-complected, not tall, not short, with teeth too big-seeming for his narrow face.

Bjarki takes a breath and tells Ethan about me and Ethan makes sure that I know his last name is without an *e* and Nate makes sure that Ethan knows that The Wood Mill is not going to pay him to talk to me and then Ethan thanks me, for what, I'm not quite sure, and I thank him too, and then he leaves.

Bjarki says, "Ethan's matured a lot since he started working here."

Nate says that Ethan does good work about 80 percent of the time.

It crosses my mind just then that maybe the fellas in the office just like to gossip and bitch.

A few weeks later, on the Saturday before Halloween, I drive to Ken's Family Restaurant, about twenty miles east of The Wood Mill, to have lunch with Ethan. In Skowhegan, I pass costumed children and parents. The *World's Tallest Indian*, a wood and metal sculpture created by Bernard Langlais, stands looking over everything, its head nearly ninety feet above the ground. Burger King, Subway, Dunks, Tractor Supply, Circle K. When I get out of the truck, there's Ethan, hands in his pockets, alone. He's wearing jeans, a baby-blue Wood Mill of Maine sweatshirt, a Nike hat.

Inside, after we've been seated at a booth, a large flat-screen TV directly behind Ethan mimics a fish tank, which has the effect of suggesting that Ethan is sitting for an underwater portrait. Red fish, blue fish, anemone, Ethan.

"It smells like sea scallops in here, that's what it smells like," Ethan says.

Over one hundred miles from the ocean, Ken's Family Restaurant specializes in seafood, the taste and smell of which Ethan finds "disgusting." Why he chose to eat here is because his aunt once washed dishes in the kitchen, though now she works at Sappi, the wood products manufacturer in Skowhegan.

On his barbecue bacon burger, Ethan requests extra pickles. He says "yup" frequently, makes eye contact but doesn't hold it. As a kid, he did some *light-logging* with his dad and uncle, but it didn't *intrigue* him. He remembers soaking-wet feet and long days punctuated by haphazardly falling trees. What he liked was playing with his brothers in the little crane, slinging wood around.

Now, at The Wood Mill, he prefers working in the yard. "It gets real repetitive, milling all the time. It's not something that intrigues me. You know, if I mess up, that's a big deal, that's twenty thousand dollars' worth of wood and I didn't even know I was a little bit off. Being out in the yard, there *is* responsibility but it's not as big a deal as being in the planing building. When I'm on the lift the whole day, I have *the* best day, especially if the sun's out." He describes a complicated method of placing packs of pine in the kiln. He talks about the height of the kiln bay, and the boom on the fork and counteracting the *tippiness* of a pack.

When I ask about those twenty-inch boards, he admits their beauty but says, "They're too plain for me. I'd rather have stuff with character, like a little blue stain."

Emphatically, Ethan does not want to work at The Wood Mill for the rest of his life. Maybe after ten or fifteen years he'll go out and get his crane operator's license. He wants to lift shipping containers on and off ocean liners. He may not like the smell of seafood, but he loves the smell of the ocean. He remembers trips to Boothbay and journeys to Cape Cod. "Oh, I loved going down to the ocean. We went crab fishing and walked out along the rock wall and we had this cool little telescope that you could stick in the water and see all the way down nice and clear. Yup. There were lots of crabs and small little fish and I didn't see anything big and I'm *glad* I didn't too because I was *swimming* in there."

Three years ago, his uncle had a tumor removed from his head. The surgery left half of his face paralyzed. "It is literally a dead cut up the middle. Sometimes, my uncle says it feels like the feeling comes back, like he's moving his face, but when he checks in the mirror, he's not. So. Yup. He wound up selling basically everything, dump trucks and the crane and stuff like that, putting out for the surgery. Boston, I guess, is crazy. My aunt gets panicky driving in the city, so my dad went down there too. For two weeks, they slept in one of the biggest carpool setups in Boston, one of those buildings where they have a bunch of parking lots on different levels—*Garage!* Yup. And then after a few people got to know them, those people went and got them food, and just *gave* it to them so they didn't even have to *pay* for it, I guess because those people respected the fact that you're living out of a car for weeks, just sitting there doing that."

He pushes the sleeves of his sweatshirt up. There is a skull with flaming eyeballs on the back of his right hand. In the future, he hopes smoke emanating from the skull's base will cover his whole arm, and the tattoos that are already there. There is a Cowboys–Yankees mashup and a gemstone mated to a set of brass knuckles. A *31*, in green, memorializes the number from his childhood football jersey. There are the names of dogs, loves, cousins. In addition, there is an abstract resembling a spiderweb, woven into a cross-hatching of vivid pink scars.

"Yup," he says. "These scars were from a bunch of knives me and my brothers used to toy around with. We used to grab butterknives. Maybe there were some steak knives in there too and I didn't realize."

Ethan's burger is barely half-eaten when his mother calls from the parking lot to tell him it's time to leave. They're going to a Halloween party tonight. Ethan will be Scorpion, a character in the video game *Mortal Kombat*. He already has a sword. Contact lenses will color his eyes yellow. He'll frighten his nieces and nephews, but, he thinks, probably not as much as his younger brother, who is going as Freddy Krueger, the serial killer who murders people in their dreams. To recreate Freddy's razor-strapped fingers, Ethan's brother duct-taped five butterknives to a work glove. It's pretty cool, Ethan says, except that Freddy doesn't have five razors—he only has four.

THIRTEEN

Spongiology

The night after Bjarki delivered the floor to Robinson Street—back in June of 2016—I lay awake on the other side of the Kennebec River, in the basement of my childhood home, obsessing over the possibility of gaps in my future. I wanted me and B to live upon a gleaming, gapless floor, a floor fit for royalty, for science, for forever. Only in retrospect can I see that I was wanting with an unreasonable passion. B and I never talked about this. What was there to talk about? I knew that perfection was crass and that a floor was just a floor and nothing more. Of course, at the same time all of that is true, none of it is true too. There were probably lots of things like this in our relationship. For instance, sometimes, when we were together, B's lips moved as if she were silently speaking with someone. Love, I suppose, is both a particle and a wave—incomprehensible, I mean—and yet, I believed I comprehended ours. B, I was sure, was mouthing the ugliest things. That's one story I tell anyway. Another involves fate, another growth, another time, another life, independence, codependence, ignorance, alcohol, dreams. I don't know. Part of me doubts everything. But that is also the part that gives no credence to time travel, so there you go.

In the basement that was so dark it made B claustrophobic, the dehumidifier beeped and whirred. We'd acquired the sleek and efficient machine because the dampness down there was affecting us personally. Towels never dried. The cat wanted out. Though the machine was filled every morning with fresh clear water, it was, metaphorically, of course, a failure. On the other hand, the newly delivered floor at Robinson Street—every floor is a relationship between individual boards and the atmosphere and the fasteners and the finish and the subfloor and the carpenter who lays the floor and the people who walk upon it—The World, that is. Relationships take time. Though temperature moves wood, water moves it more. Wood moves ten times more across the grain than with it, widthwise as opposed to lengthwise. Nails keep boards flat, but not immobile, and floors that are silent in winter will talk in summer. Ditto: doors. Ditto: people.

There's a story about a floor under a leaking roof. The leak creates a puddle and the puddle spreads across the floor, which acts like a sponge, absorbing all that water. As the wood swells, the sponge becomes a bulldozer, expanding so much that it pushes the walls—the vertical exterior stud walls—right off the foundation: a floor knocking its own house down. I can't remember if B was lying next to me that night, and if she was, how much space was or wasn't between us. We'd met on opposite sides of a crowded booth and told ghost stories. Perhaps we had never been next to each other. Perhaps we will never not be. And who are we? "Due to our strict kiln-drying specification," The Wood Mill Installation Guide reads, "our white pine will act like a sponge." Sponges evolved six hundred million years ago, in nutrient-starved environments. They are animals, not plants, relying on the flow of water to deliver food and oxygen. It's called *spongiology*. An animal is an animal because of something to do with cell walls, locomotion, embryonic development, and several other specific things I do not fully understand. I am an animal. A loofah is a vegetable in the cucumber family. I was raised by vegetarians. A cucumber is a cucumber. Like I said, though I had only a vague understanding of what this all meant, I believed my understanding was absolute. I had installed all kinds of floors—*laid* them—oak, maple, fir, birch, bamboo, click-clack, tile, and pine too, two-hundred-year-old stuff as well as your standard NeLMA variety. I was supremely confident, I mean, and at the same time I have always been afraid of the dark.

Wood, as we know, my love, is hygroscopic. Seeking equilibrium with the air, it breathes. It breathes water in, and it breathes water out, expanding and contracting until it reaches what is known as its equilibrium moisture content (EMC). (EMC, a function partially of humidity, is always changing.) (You could argue that there is no such thing as EMC.) (You can argue anything you want.) Maybe you've had occasion to observe a board respiring on your sunny lawn? The board's lawn-side will absorb moisture while the non-lawn-side will lose moisture. The bottom of the board will expand while the top shrinks. The result: a board curling away from the grass, cupping. Abracadabra. A radius is longer than a line. Even just one humid day, Nate says, will cause a kiln-dried board to pop; he eats Rice Krispies with sugar spooned on top.

When we enter the kiln, it is 110 degrees inside, the humidity near 100 percent.

"It's like a freaking rainforest in here," Nate says.

The kiln is divided into two chambers, each capable of holding about twelve packs of lumber. Pine boards in stickered packs are stacked from floor to ceiling. It is said that a one-inch-thick pine board left out to dry will season in one year. In the kiln, the same board, no matter the width, will dry in two weeks. By then, the amount of water in the wood (the wood's moisture content, or MC) will be around 6.5 percent, or about half that of your common kiln-dried NeLMA board. (Depending on the season, location, and species, a freshly cut log may have an MC between 45 and 200 percent. The water (or ice) may weigh twice as much as the wood. (But what is wood?))

In the kiln, most of a board's moisture is removed at the beginning of the two-week drying cycle. That's the easy water. During the last week, the temperature is increased about 5 degrees per day until it reaches about 160 degrees Fahrenheit. After fourteen days, a board has lost significant heft.

From a load of boards, Nate says, "I could easily remove a gallon of water a minute."

A similar phenomenon can be observed in the forest. Hot days dehydrate trees. The needles of white pines grow in bundles of five. Each needle is as long as my pinky finger and sharp to the touch. Every two years, a white pine will replace all of its needles. (Every day, you will replace about 330 billion of your 30 trillion cells.) If you were covered in needles, you'd photosynthesize too. That would be cool. Photosynthesis and trees are cool, obviously. A *Pinus strobus* needle, in cross section, is triangular. Microscopic openings called *stomata* allow respiration of carbon dioxide and oxygen and water vapor. Evaporating water creates a kind of suction, drawing more water up from the roots. This occurs because of capillary action, which has something to do with surface tension and the hydrogen bonds connecting water molecules, which may or may not be the same thing. I'm talking here about the movement of xylem sap. Phloem sap moves photosynthate down from the needles, from nutrient *source* to *sink*, flowing between the cambium and the bark. Xylem sap flows through sapwood. Water up, water down. Can a sponge do that? Consider the straw instead—innumerable straws, bundled to form a tree's trunk. In a pine tree, these straws are tracheid cells, three to five millimeters long and twenty-five to thirty-five microns in diameter. A micron is just another way of saying micrometer. One micron is equal to one-millionth of a meter. A human hair is about seventy-five microns in diameter. Magnify the cut end of a pine board twenty times and you'll see something like a honeycomb of straws. These are the cut ends of tracheids. Diameter varies. The more densely concentrated straws are the late wood and the larger straws are the early wood. (In each tracheid, there is a primary cell wall and a secondary cell wall. The secondary wall has three layers. Each layer is composed of cellulose polymer chains known as microfibrils. (Put a bunch of glucose molecules together and you get cellulose.) (Photosynthesis produces glucose.) (Cellulose, which is indigestible, is sometimes added to foods. Microcrystalline cellulose (MCC), "powdered cellulose," methylcellulose, cellulose gum. It's in shredded cheeses, preventing clumping. It adds creaminess to ice cream. Enjoy it in your McDonald's fish fillets, chicken strips, biscuits.) $(C_6H_{10}O_5)$ (Lignin, an amorphous polymer, helps hold everything together.)) Actually, a tracheid is shaped more like a very elongated diamond, not like a straw at all. Manhole-like structures dot its sides. These "pits" connect adjacent tracheids, enabling the flow of water. Because water in a tree is essential for photosynthesis and also for maintaining turgor in the cells, the more water a tree can transport, the faster it will grow. This, however, is not always beneficial. Fast-growing trees are more susceptible to heat and drought.

Consider for a moment a single tracheid within a single board. It's been a straw and it's been a diamond and it's been a sponge and now it's a bottle. Whether any bottle in a board is full or empty, it is always the same bottle shape and bottle size. That's just how trees are. But the unique thing about our bottle (tracheid) is that its walls are also capable of holding moisture— bound water. When the walls cannot hold any more moisture, the bottle (tracheid) is said to be at its fiber saturation point (FSP). It is only after this *bound water* begins to evaporate that the bottle will shrink. Imagine millions of bottles, billions, each of them shrinking (and swelling), shrinking (and swelling) at different rates along each axis. (An eastern white pine tracheid dried from its FSP (green) to an MC of 0 percent (oven-dry) will shrink 6.1 percent tangentially, 2.1 percent radially, and about 0.15 percent longitudinally.)

I mean, it's not like I *really* care about the gaps in your floor, or that I think a world made only of gapless floors is A Better World, but at the same time, I *do*. I do care. A marriage could never be built upon a gappy floor. Imagine the splinters and stubbed toes and recriminations, the buttons and coins and connections lost to those abysmal black separations. I mean, that's what I thought then. Now, even as caring less can seem like a kind of giving up, I also like to think of it as a different kind of giving, a good kind, though *when* and *how much* drives even the chickadees crazy.

FOURTEEN

Shavings (The Thirty-Seventh View)

The first time I walked into the planer building, the doorknob fell off. It was a brutally cold day in January of 2017 and the plumbing was frozen solid. I remember standing before a snowbank, noting my own clarity next to several yellow patches of dehydration and I remember thinking that this was significant, though not because it indicated my own secret elitism.

Today, a hot summer day, Hunter calls the bathroom *the coolest spot at The Mill.*

Today, Nate calls it *the think tank.*

Today, because there are several dead mice in the grime-ringed bathtub, Bjarki calls it *the murder room.* A poisoned mouse, bleeding inside, dies thirsty. I've been told that it's not a good idea to drink the water from the tap. Beside the sink, on the spotless pine vanity, there's a dispenser of Orange Goop hand cleaner. A paperback by Bob Fenster, *Duh! The Stupid History of the Human Race.* When you look in the mirror, you see what you see in the mirror.

But the planer—the planer is like the oven in the kitchen, the engine under the hood, the heart in your chest. The band saw is beside it and the straight-line rip saw beside that. Wind gusts through the three bay doors that open every direction but west, rattling straps and bands, rolling bottles and cans, raising dust and grit and shavings in a billowing storm that swirls around the frames of safety glasses. A nest of discarded stickers on the concrete floor. Bunks. Roller stands. The steel framed-in feed table with its wheels and teeth and appendages, its ratty conveyor, and on the conveyor, a board, and then another board, and then another, end to end to end they go, west to east, no gaps between, thirty-two feet per minute on the pre-size, half that speed on the final finish pass.

"Right at the end of yesterday it stopped. It's like, 'That's *weird*. That smells *bad*.' Then, this morning, it turned right on—*Awesome!*—and then it was like *burrrbur bur. Bur*—'Fuck!' I called The Guy and he had a motor and I put it in and fired it up and it was going really slow, *the wrong direction,* so

I swapped two wires and it *still* went the wrong way and I was like, 'That's weird,' so I called The Guy and he was like, 'That means you don't have a leg.'"

Five motors, between fifteen and twenty horsepower, run this Portuguese-made Pinheiro. Under the hood, see the chain drives and the metal wheels and the hold-downs and the straight twenty-five-inch knives and so much more that you do not understand.

"It looks like it could power a submarine." I, who has never seen a submarine, say that.

"Do I get to proofread this before it gets published?"

This is this, what you're reading now, The Book.

With a fork, Hunter delivers a pack of kiln-dried pine ready for pre-sizing.

With a fork, Hunter delivers a pack of pre-sized pine ready for finish planing.

Pre-sizing happens after the kiln-drying, before the straight-lining. The finish pass cuts the tongue and the groove. We'll get to all that.

"I'm trying to teach you good work ethics and so far you're getting like a D."

(The day Ethan quit for good, shortly after seven in the morning, he called Bjarki. He was crying.)

Everyone either has their sleeves rolled up or doesn't have sleeves. Nate shaves his armpits to improve ventilation. Hunter applies Old Spice. Summer sweat disappears into ankle-deep shavings. Nutmeg and lemons. A Red Bull floats by. An empty container of nondetergent motor oil. A snow shovel.

"We've got a *fuck ton* of tongue and groove to do today."

"You have the American ton, the metric ton, and then the *fuck ton*."

"The Maine measuring system."

"*Price Is Right* rules and you would have won."

Each Wood Mill floor is planed specifically for each customer. As Hunter and Nate build an order, they guess the lengths of boards. A tape measure officiates. The boards shine.

"That's mill sheen," Nate says. With a black Sharpie, he writes FREE on the end of a board marred by stop-and-go marks, glossy lines across the board's width: mill sheen in concentrated form.

But the planer—it will tell you things if you listen, about knots and cupping and twist, bits of metal, deviations in thickness, dull knives, loose knives, love.

"Your coffee's getting cold."

"Why?"

"Because you're not drinking it."

"What?"

"What?"

"I thought you said 'The office is getting old.'"

"Your book should have a disclaimer about quote accuracy."

About quote, accuracy, or the accuracy of the quotes?

"Say you're rich and have a butler. You hold up a teeny bell and ring it over your head. Picture that but with your index finger as the bell. That's the nicked knife signal."

Pine sucks up minerals and grit as it grows. Trees are pelted with lead and tungsten and copper, errant bird shot and buckshot and bullets. The finest specimens that have passed through the planer—disfigured metallic mushrooms with one gleaming flat surface—they are preserved in a drawer.

Nate leaps onto the infeed conveyor, walks it like a plank, feeds himself to the planer.

"We used to call this Indian-style," he says. "People take things too seriously. Words don't *mean* anything. I mean, they do *and* they don't. I don't care if you want to be a girl or a boy—either is great. Whatever. You be you. But how am I supposed to know—" A slight interruption in the dust on the knife's edge reveals the nick. Nate's fingernail confirms it. Moments earlier, along the length of the last planed board, a raised line finer than any capellini was the first indication. Hunter, the outfeed man, felt it, rang the bell for the butler.

Nate slides a stone across the knife. The hood of the planer, propped open with a slim piece of oak, appears poised to snap shut.

"I'm in a mousetrap," he says.

Shavings stick to my socks, shimmy into my boots, crater with each step.

The sun slanting in through the south bay door like day's-end optimism.

Flexible ducts snorkeling up from the planer. Rigid metal ducts painted yellow, wrapped in red tape, flaking rust.

Menno comes inside from one of the shavings trailers out back, tarred and shaved.

Menno, in a corner, snips used metal straps.

Menno, in the yard, pulls his cart with its metal wheels.

"I could invest I don't know how many hundreds of thousands of dollars on computers and equipment to speed things up, but that's not who we are. That's not what we do. We'd have to move way more volume. Quality would go down. Plus, people who shop with us love how low tech and stripped down the machinery is. It reminds them of their grandfather's old shop. Plus, Nate is a true craftsman. He knows more than any computer."

A green wheel to adjust height, thickness, depth, width, speed, angles. A wheel on nearly every machine. Sometimes more than one. Calipers and metal rulers to double-check. A two-by-four wedged to fix a flimsy clamp. Yellow fiberglass insulation from a mouse's nest. Here's a stack of planed walnut. A stack of un-planed cherry. That's birch. Flooring for Colby College. Pine for South Carolina. Pine for a Quaker. Pine for a Trumper, for the governor's brother, for Durham, the Vineyard. Pine from New York, from Vermont, from Maine. Where are all these flies from?

They're circling above a stack of poplar.

Nate says, *popple*.

The poplar, awaiting its tongue and its groove, says nothing.

Beside us, Ethan is measuring poplar boards.

"What's the *narrowest*?"

"Seven and three-quarters is your average."

"Is that the *smallest*?"

"Yeah."

"Then that's not the average. That's the *smallest*."

Nate calls the flies horseflies.

I ask if Mercer ever sees greenheads. It's a weird way of framing the question. Show me what is not non sequitur. Define *gap*. *Tabanus nigrovittatus* belongs to a family of biters, your horseflies and moose flies, all of which are known as pool-feeders. (There may be as many as 350 species of tabanid in North America.) (Those triangular deer flies actually belong to the genus *Chrysops*.) *Biting* may not be the most accurate locution. Their heads aren't actually green. It's their disproportionate, iridescent eyes. (Only 2 percent of the human population has green eyes.) Fly eyes are *compound*, consisting of thousands of apertures called ommatidia. The resolution is poor, but your angle of view is wide. See the buffet of sunbathers on the sand. After pupating in the adjacent salt marsh, you have fed exclusively on sugary substances, like nectar. You have laid your first eggs and now you seek blood, for blood will allow you to reproduce again. You alight on pink flesh, pinch skin, slice microscopic capillaries. The blood pools. You don't lick or suck, exactly, but through the myriad "food channels" in your labella, you absorb me like a sponge.

"And I don't want to be like—"

"Or."

"You know?"

"But."

"I mean."

"Nate, Nate, Nate, do you copy?"

"No, I know. I could have a best friend, and we could have *everything* in common, but after two or three days, it's like, 'Get away from me!'"

"Yeah."

"So—?"

"So I don't know what's going on."

"So that kind of sucks, but at the same time not."

"Yeah," I say. "Both."

FIFTEEN

3:04 in the Afternoon

"Planing," Nate says ironically, obviously, "is one of life's great mysteries. The board goes in. The board comes out." He is standing at the east end of the planer building, by the bay door, which is open. Between Nate and the planer is the outfeed table, a polished metal surface about as tall as your local bar-top and about as wide. It's maybe ten feet long. The actual length of the table is important because the table is not any other length than its actual length, which I don't know exactly. You can only ask so many questions. On the other side of the table, perpendicular to it, are several stacks of pine. Nate is building a floor destined for Durham, Maine. He pulls a board and pushes a circular saw through it. Underfoot are short lengths of twelve-inch-wide tongue and groove pine, the discarded cutoffs from finished floorboards.

"The planer's running like shit today," he says.

Why?

"If I *knew why*, it wouldn't be running like shit."

One of life's great mysteries.

A series of polished imprints span the width of one board. Each is a stop-and-go mark, a blemish indicating a pause in the board's passage through the planer.

"That's where the knife is just sitting there, hanging out."

By sitting there, hanging out, he means spinning at a rate of about 5,500 revolutions per minute.

Hunter says, "Flooring always runs good until I get here."

Nate says, "That's true too."

On the Durham pack, Nate fits two boards together, tongue into groove. "Technically, these boards are fine. I have no qualms or gripes if you do a whole floor with stop-and-go marks and then sand it. No one would ever know, but visually, right now, I don't like it. You can make everything *almost* unnoticeable, but if you really look. . . . When you take a board out in the sun, you will always see something. Things pop in the sun."

Hunter says, "Some guy just showed up. I swore he was a woman until he talked to me."

Nate says, "There was an episode of *Maury* with a total bearded woman. That's what her job was, to be a woman with a scraggly-ass beard. Apparently, certain women grow beards. Some women shave, but she let hers grow."

"Nate, Nate, Nate."

Hunter says, "Why does everyone show up at lunchtime?"

Nate says, "Everyone does."

He sweeps a freshly planed Durham board with his hand, pushes a knot, glances at another. "If you can feel the knot, it's going to come out. Just because it's small, doesn't mean it's going to stay. A red or maroon knot will never come out. That was a living branch. A black ring around a maroon knot is coming out. That's a branch that died recently. A small black knot rarely comes out. That's a branch that's been dead a while. But most people don't actually want perfectly clear boards. They want knots. It's like the clarity of a diamond."

"Nate, Nate, Nate."

"Um, go grab like twenty twelve-inch boards and then we'll go to lunch."

Hunter stands there, grinning.

Nate claps his hands. "Chop, chop." (As a consequence of operating the straight-line rip saw, Nate—himself—has become two men. It's not that he has been cut in two, as all the boards passed through the saw are cut in two; it's that he is now both the outfeed man *and* the infeed man. What Nate says is, "Depending on *who* the outfeed man is, the outfeed man just slows me down." Nate does not slow Nate down. A straight-line rip saw is a type of table saw. The fifteen-inch-diameter blade spins, but it doesn't move, if you know what I mean. The boards move. Sixty carbide-tipped teeth saw the wood, ripping. The temperature in the planer building is not more than 20 degrees. (It would have been perfect (for The Book) if Nate was straight-line-ripping the twelve-inchers for Durham that I will watch him plane months later, but he is not. And it would have been perfect (for The Book) if he was ripping those twenties that I'm writing about, but he is not—all of which I suppose actually *is* perfect, in a way. (While it is true that a twenty-inch board is ripped and planed exactly like every other board, it is of course also not true.)) Nate is sorting through a head-high stack of boards between ten and eighteen inches wide, all of them pre-sized. A pre-sized board has been sawn from a log, kiln-dried, and then passed once through The Wood Mill's planer. The pre-size pass planes to a uniform thickness of fifteen-sixteenths of an inch. This pass through the planer "cleans up" (planes) the two surfaces of each board so that the infeed man on the straight-line rip saw (Nate) can grade the boards more easily. It also lightens the boards. The grades today are junk and crate and floor. *Junk*, apparently, is synonymous with *shit* and *kindling* and *fence*. *Crate* is synonymous with *shit*, though a slightly higher grade than *kindling* or *fence*. At almost any other mill, a crate board could be a floorboard. At The Wood Mill, a finished crate board is seven and a quarter inches wide. ("How many of those little notebooks have you filled up?") Nate flips a board from the head-high stack and throws it into a spin reminiscent of a figure skater.

(Winter sunlight like some idealized version of light itself.)

"See," he says, "this board is one side good, one side bad."

He sets the board on the deck of the saw, then takes its tail lightly. Several wheels pin the board to a metal conveyor, which receives the board from Nate's hands and, in a straight line, ushers it forward so that the saw rips the sixteen-foot-long board.

Bahahahaha.

A seven-and-a-quarter-inch board drops into the outfeed man's (Nate's) hands. The remainder of the original board—nine inches wide now—is still pinned, extending beyond the saw like a diving board just dived from, wagging. The conveyor conveys nothing. The saw saws nothing. The dust collection collects nothing. (*Nothing* is not true.) (Nothing is *not true*.) (There is a special kind of endurance involved with repetitive manual labor. "Let your mind wander. Think of movies, shows, dinner, jokes, memories, anything. Or just look at the grain and knots. Pine is pretty good for character. I saw Jimmy Durante in a knot once. *Cha cha cha*. Mickey Mouse and cock and balls show up regularly too. I've saved the end of a board that looked like a turkey and a couple of knots that looked like dueling pistols and a foot-long knot that looked like a trout. When I saw Jesus, I hung him up in the break room.") Nate slides the now-nine-inch-wide board back over the deck of the saw, walks to the infeed side of things, takes the board, and, hand over hand, presents it to the conveyor. He is bringing into being things that before were not. He is creating. The world is changing.

Bahahahaha. The nine becomes a seven and a two. Approximately. The width of the saw blade, the kerf, is about an eighth of an inch. About an eighth of an inch of what was a nine-inch board is now dust.

How many boards are in a pack of crate boards?

One hundred, Nate says. Seventeen layers, six boards wide.

Wool, technically, one hundred and *two*, but one hundred is simpler.

Bahahahahaha. A fourteen becomes a seven and a quarter and a six.

"If I was going to describe that board, I would go—" Nate's whistle inflects as his right hand mimics a kind of swan curve. "It's a little bit of—" He whistles again.

Bahahahaha.

"This one is pretty much a piece of shit."

"This is a giant piece of shit."

"Junk."

Who bought the logs that became these boards?

Nate bought the good ones.

Only about half of the board feet that The Wood Mill purchases in log form become board feet in board form. Straight-lining, Nate says, is about "maximizing yield."

Hunter, the outfeed man now, holds up six gloved fingers, indicating ninety-six boards in the pack.) You return to the planer building a couple hours after lunch, shortly before three in the afternoon. The twelve-inch boards Hunter has retrieved—the last boards for Durham—are on the scissor lift. There is a single stationary board in the planer, halfway in, halfway out. The planer is off. Maybe eight feet of the board rests on the infeed table. The infeed table is basically a conveyor belt. On the other side of the planer, the outfeed side, the same board extends a few feet. So not *halfway* at all. On the infeed side, the board is fifteen-sixteenths of an inch thick and twelve and a quarter inches wide. On the outfeed side, the board is three-quarters of an inch thick with a tongue cut into one edge and a groove in the other. The tongue is fifteen-thousandths of an inch narrower than the groove, about half the thickness of your fingernail. ("I don't believe in heaven," Nate says.) The face of the board measures eleven and a half inches. This does not include the tongue. Does your face include a tongue? The tongue points north. (I asked Nate once if he thought the board emerging from the planer was the same board that went in.

Nate: Same board. Just a little flatter, and smoother

Matthew: So it's a different board!

Nate: Haha. More like cosmetic surgery

Matthew: New face, new you!

Nate: New, but better [smiling emoji]

Matthew: Exactly! The same but not!)

(The modern handplane originated thousands of years ago when a chisel was fixed to a block of wood. (This happened in Europe and also in Asia.) As time passes, handles are added to the tool, as well as means to adjust the blade. The block of wood gets wider, longer, thinner, becomes metal. The cutting knife improves. Some planes remove large swaths of wood, others fine ribbons. Some address end-grain or miters. They bevel, rabbet, joint, and bead. They tongue and they groove and they smooth. Imagine the surface of a board as if it were the surface of the sea. Looked at from the side, there are crests and troughs, high spots and low spots. To flatten the sea, the crests must be cut down until all the troughs are in a single plane. Your boat has a knife protruding from the keel, shaving waves as it sails.)

Do I want to know anything before you start the planer?

I want to know *everything*.

You say, "Hopefully, it runs."

And then, "No. It's like anything: someone can tell you all day until they're blue in the face *why this* and *why that* but until *you* actually do it, that's when you understand."

A fly the size of a jumbo jet materializes near us—that's what the planer sounds like (to me (I have never actually heard a fly the size of a jumbo jet (except in my mind))). It's about 3:01 p.m. The board partway through the planer, which is properly called a *blank*, but which I will be calling The Board, doesn't move—perceptibly, that is. The conveyor belt on the infeed table doesn't move perceptibly. The fly is more like a hornet. (A *blank* is a board that has been kiln-dried, pre-sized, and straight-lined. It has not yet gone through the planer on the finish pass, not yet received a tongue and a groove. Blanks of only one width are passed through the planer at a certain time. (This afternoon it's all twelves.)) The infeed table was fabricated to handle everything from square timbers to floorboards, specifically for The Wood Mill, specifically for a right-handed operator. You are that right-handed operator. Your fabric gloves have been dipped in blue latex. (One pair of gloves becomes holey in one week.) (Latex comes from trees.) ("As far as any job goes, you should always do it the best you can. I don't care whether you're a cashier or a garbage man. If the garbage spills and there's goop everywhere—pick it up. Have a little pride. But, no, I don't think of it as fixing the world, so to speak."

Is there any job Nate would be unwilling to do?

"No matter how gross a job is, once you do it long enough, it becomes the norm."

"What about ethically?"

"Like a lawyer working for a nuclear company wanting to dump shit everywhere?"

"Or selling weapons."

"Who am I selling to?"

"The bad guys."

"Let me see how to word this—say I'm the *only* one selling weapons to the bad guys, then definitely, no. But if they were going to get them from someplace else anyway. . . . But I also feel like I'd tell the FBI so that they could go fuck the bad guys.") Above the end of the conveyor is a small metal wheel. Blunt ridges mark its circumference, providing traction. This is the infeed roller. It turns clockwise in space. With your right hand, you flip a switch. A pneumatic piston hisses. The infeed roller lowers to The Board, turns a fraction, and then stops. The Board continues to not move. Ditto the conveyor. Hydraulics power everything.

It's water, you say.

The roller goes up and the roller goes down. *Psst, psst.* Air. Water. You. The smallest things without warning move me. Behind the conveyor, mounted to the machine, is a row of steel studs evenly spaced inches apart, a couple dozen thumbs up. You grasp a steel wrecking bar that I had not seen, that did not exist for me until I saw you take it up, that. . . . How much of the world is like this? You position the bar's end between two "teeth" or "thumbs" or "studs" or "prying nubs" and then you leverage the bar against The Board (Though you don't know him as Two Teeth, you remember him.). The Board moves forward a few inches. The hornet dances. The jet revs. A stop-and-go mark polished. You pry again and again. You appear to be rowing.

It is approximately 3:03 p.m. I look toward Hunter, the outfeed man, to gauge what is going on with you and The Board. Inscribed across his hooded sweatshirt is the word CHAMPION. He's wearing brown Carhartt jeans, gloves, a grin, two hats—a black winter hat over a gray brimmed hat. (Two hours prior, right after lunch, Hunter hopped into the new forklift with the heated cab to unload a waiting tractor trailer of six-by-sixes. Operating a fork is simple, he said. "You move the lever up to go down and the lever down to go up."

As I followed Hunter and the fork and his two hats across the yard, Menno walked beside me. He must have heard me saying something at lunch about the holes in my teeth because he said, "I myself have never been to the dentist."

I said I ate a lot of sugar, which was true.

"Oh, I eat a lot of sugar too," he said.

The sky was so blue and the sun was so warm and it felt so good to be out in it. A radio clipped to the front of Menno's jacket looked very big there. In September, his family had come to Maine on a train. They'd raised produce in Ohio and recycled materials from old barns and made windowsills from sassafras. He said it again, *sassafras*. Now his family owned 180 acres in Mercer. He said, "There are eighteen of us kids so we can do a lot of things."

When Menno excused himself to help a customer, Hunter told me to ask him to tell a certain joke when he came back. The incident with the UPS guy was in my mind then and I did not want to put Menno in a similar situation. (In the office, Nate suggests I ask the UPS guy to tell the dirtiest joke he knows.

I say, "Tell the dirtiest joke you know."

The UPS guy says, "How do you get a Mexican girl pregnant?") Still, I figured an Amish joke—I don't know what I was thinking—couldn't be that bad.

Okay. So these old guys go ice fishing and all morning they're not catching shit—Menno said that, *shit*—and they see a kid just pulling 'em up, pulling 'em up, and the old men go ask the kid how he's catching all those fish and the kid says, *Mumglemumbruh*—something incomprehensible—and the men are like, *What?* cupping their ears, and the kid lifts a finger like, *hold on*, and then he spits out a mouthful of worms and says, *You gotta keep the worms warm.*

This wasn't the joke Hunter had in mind.

"*You* tell it," Menno said.

Menno had been on my right side but now he was on my left.

He said, "Well, have you ever written a book before?"

Hunter said, "I wrote one story for school about a battle between owls and eagles. It was like twenty pages long and every day I'd add more onto it."

Menno said, "I read so many books. I like the Hardy Boys, anything that gets you on the edge of your seat. But I read mostly Anabaptist books and also Civil War books. I like history. I like to see how I was."

I asked him to repeat himself and he said it again, "I like to see how I was."

Hunter said he was an avid hunter but that he disliked hunting with rifles. He hunted deer with a compound bow.

Menno had shot deer with a crossbow.

Hunter said a crossbow might as well be a rifle. He asked if Menno wanted to hunt coyotes later and Menno said yes and I asked Hunter why he liked shooting coyotes and he said, "Coyotes are something I can shoot year round. Killing them keeps the deer alive."

That grin—I couldn't read it at all. I asked about pronunciation.

Hunter said, "*Ki-yote, yote, ki-yoatee, dog.*"

We were squinting so hard in the sunlight we couldn't help but grin.

"It's not a joke for a book," Menno said.)

Bpbpbpbpb. You blow out through your lips. *Motorboating,* we said growing up. You raise and lower the infeed roller, raise and lower the infeed roller. *Psst, psst. Psst, psst.* Nothing. Gripping The Board, you lean the full force of your body toward the planer. Still The Board does not move. *Psst, psst.* (Running like shit.) When you turn your face I see the shadow of a beard, which I don't remember from this morning. You pick up a narrower, junkier board and place it on the infeed table, directly behind The Board. By *junkier* I just

mean not a future floorboard. With the steel bar, you row this board forward, forcing The Board through the planer a few inches at a time. When the tail of The Board has nearly disappeared into the planer, you raise the infeed roller—*psst*—set the junk board aside, and place a fresh twelve-inch blank on the infeed conveyor. You know exactly why you do this. The conveyor conveys the blank until it encounters the end of The Board. *Psst, psst*. You sigh. The sun slanting through the south bay door suggests the interior of a precious stone. You walk to the end of the situation, to the tail of the blank, retrieve a hefty bunk from the floor. Hanging from the end of the conveyor table is a loop of strapping, the wide woven kind. Follow a line long enough and eventually it will become a circle. (Nate says, "Why *are* you on this planet? Why am *I* on this planet?") With your chest, you pin the bunk to the butt of the blank. You grip the strap, take a breath, stare down the length of the blank to The Board. The first thing a board encounters as it disappears into what I am for some reason calling the maw of the planer is the top feed roll, which is essentially several feed rollers aligned end to end. These grip the board and pull it deeper into the machine. Ahead and below, a cylinder spins at a rate of about 5,500 rotations per minute. That's a little more than ninety rotations per second. Fixed on opposite sides of this cutter head are two knives twenty-five inches long. Only one of the knives cuts. During the finish pass through the planer (when everything is running smoothly), boards travel at about sixteen feet per minute, or three inches per second. One spinning knife encounters a single inch of floorboard about thirty times. Interestingly, the two knives in the cutter head spend the entirety of their working lives together. A pair is never separated. Don't say *married*. They spin together and are sharpened together and, as a result, match each other nearly exactly in mass. (Car tires are balanced too.) The middle and then the third feed roller ushers the board deeper. A pressure bar keeps the board pinned flat. A chip breaker directs shavings toward the ductwork. (Early in his tenure at The Wood Mill, Nate once set the planer knives out of line by two-thousandths of an inch, a nearly imperceptible amount. When Nate asked his supervisor if that was good enough, the man replied, "I don't know. Do you want your work to be two-thousandths off?") ("Knives," Nate says, "won't make machines run bad unless they're dull as fuck.") (A top or a bottom knife might plane 15,000 feet of pine before it requires sharpening.) (Nate says, "K lopped his fingers off. That wasn't bad. There was a stick in the duct, just there, not doing anything. When K grabbed the stick, the side head hit the stick and sucked his hand in and took off the first knuckle of his middle finger and just above the knuckle on his ring finger. I heard a snap. I didn't know if it was the wood or K's hand.") Above the board now is the top head, spinning two knives. Now the top and the bottom faces of the board are flat and parallel; the thickness—three-quarters of an inch—is set. The side heads, though configured differently than the top and bottom heads, spin at the same rate, cutting the tongue on one side and the groove on the other. (It's almost 3:30. The goal is to have blanks moving continuously through the planer, without gaps between. Gaps waste time. Time costs money. There are four stacks of five boards on the scissor lift. Nate lifts a blank, turns it on edge, turns it over, turns it back. His movements are similar but not always the same, dictated by a framework of calculations and considerations made instantly and unconsciously. There are only four possible orientations in which a board can pass through the planer and only one of them is right. "Cupping trumps all," Nate says. A cup is a bow across the width of the board. Not many boards are cupped at this point in the milling process (the finish pass) but if one is, the top of the bow (the crown) must become the top of the board. Cup down. Crown up. "If I put the board through upside down like a *U*, it's almost like a bird flapping its wings." Nate lifts the edge of a blank to his right eye, his dominant eye. A *sweepy* board is curved like a parenthesis. Though the planer can eliminate up to a quarter inch of sweep, no boards at The Wood Mill should express sweep of more than an eighth of an inch. (A carpenter, with wedges, chisel, hammer, clamps, levers, and whatever else, should be able to flex most sweep from most floorboards. There's not much to be done when boards get wider than twelve inches, not much except accept the gap, or cut out the sweep, or chuck the board.) (Nate can see sweep as subtle as one thirty-second of an inch in sixteen feet.) (By the south bay door, the lowering sun magnified in metallic reflection.) Nate eases the board from his eye and then drops it so that the board almost bounces back into his gloved hand. In a novice, these movements might be made in a rush to achieve gaplessness, but Nate is unhurried and the intricacies of each gesture disappear into a kind of flowing progress. Large mills employ robots and artificial intelligence to do what Nate does. (Bjarki says, "There is no one else who does what we do. I know mills that can shove wood through a planer, but to have boards come out right, it's tricky."

He mentions one mill. He says, "I wouldn't send my worst enemy there."

Nate says, "Fuck those people."

"They don't know how to plane wood."

"They work off of volume and speed. It's like, 'Hey, we did ten thousand feet today. It looks all fucked-up and gross, but hey, we did it.'") ("My brain says, 'Okay, this should work,' so I flip it and at the same time look at the other side and if it's considerably nicer than the side I saw first I spin it but if I flip it and it's either worse or the same I'll leave it.") (The speed of light as represented by the constant, *c*.) (*Let Us Now Praise*—.) Sometimes, the combination of sweep and cup and grade requires Nate to helicopter a blank, to turn it end for end. This may be the only moment when Nate carries a board's full weight. All of his movements—sliding, pivoting, leveraging, sharing the board with a roller stand, the infeed table, the stack of wood—minimize his load. (Physically, he says, the most exhausting days are pre-sizing days, when he might run five thousand linear feet through the planer.) (There is a distinction to be made between lineal and linear, but it's probably not

important here.) (A twenty-inch board weighs twice as much as a ten-inch board.) Nate lifts the twelve-inch blank to shoulder height, to head height. He rolls one edge up, but not all the way up, spinning and stepping the whole time. ("Technically, if there are a hundred boards, I could helicopter all one hundred to keep the sweep right.") (I believe the figure of speech concerns a bull pirouetting in a china shop.) ("As far as life goes, try to enjoy it, and don't be a raging dickhole, and try not to be dumb as fuck. There is no *meaning*. What *you* want to do is different from what *I* want to do. I don't want to say there is no purpose—but if you're running a race, the purpose is to win. In life you don't really *win*. Everyone dies."

What about Jeff Bezos, or Donald Trump, or Michael Jordan?

"They maybe have accomplished what they wanted to accomplish, but that doesn't mean they have more fun or are happier than me. It all depends on how you *view* stuff. I'm very scientific. We're just here because we're here. My mom and dad had sex. I was formed. I came out. It's hard to explain. My life is just, like. . . . Hey, if something pops up, I try to fix it. I go to work, come home, hang out with my kids, and try to make sure they're not going to become the dicks of society. When I get old and they are happy and nice people, I'll feel as though I did a good job. Whether or not that's my *purpose*, I don't know.") He lowers the blank and twitches it onto the conveyor. He pulls it forward to meet the end of the blank already moving through the planer, no gaps between, the parenthesis about to be removed. (On a good day, three thousand linear feet of finished flooring will emerge from the planer.)) Your cheeks swell. Your face reddens. When you pull the strap, you are really pulling your body forward, forcing the bunk that is pinned across your chest against the blank so that it pushes The Board, The Board which is indubitably stuck. The loop in the strap is now a line. Your feet slip backward. You grew up in Industry, in a house your father and his friends built. There were a couple of springs and streams back there on the mountain that you'd go unclog and make a nice trench for the water to go in, you know what I mean, so that the water just flowed and then you'd build a little lean-to like a fort and hang out there and then you'd go build another one. Your favorite spot was where this one tree grew right up from a stream bank carved out by the water so that the trunk was normal aboveground or whatever but then all the roots were exposed below. The roots formed this cool cave and you played beneath the roots that were dripping after it rained or just like if it was misty and when the roots were wet, they were black. (On the phone, Nate says, "*Dog*! Go away. Go *lay* down. Wrong way. Opposite way." He says, "Crazy dog. Usually my dad would yell at me and be like 'Nate!' and I'd be like, 'What!' and he'd be like, 'Just checking!'") ("It was a pine tree.") At 3:03:50 p.m., the bunk shifts on your chest and you release the strap and let out your breath and move to put the bunk aside. But you do not put the bunk aside. Again you pin the bunk with your chest to the blank's end. The tension between your body, the bunk, the blank, The Board, and the machine seems liable to snap at any moment. It is not a joke for a book. Again you pull in order to push. You pull again in order to push. You pull in order to push again.

SIXTEEN

Shavings (Real America (Afterward))

Now, if I were to ask you, seriously, how a Mexican woman (or girl) might become pregnant, I'm sure you'd say the very same way every woman becomes pregnant.

I say, "I have no idea."

The UPS guy says how.

It takes a moment to orient to this new information and then we groan, laugh, applaud.

The UPS guy tells one about a clitoris and a Bud Light.

Another about rainbow trout and Skittles.

It's months before the insurrection. UPS stops by every afternoon.

"Good afternoon, The Wood Mill."

Nate leans toward me and says, "What's the definition of disgusting?"

The definition of disgusting, apparently, involves your grandmother and some confusion about a specific number of oysters.

"B-j-a-r-k-i ... *beee-arky.*"

Nate asks if I'm writing down the definition of disgusting.

I say, "I remember one time I was in here and Bjarki said to you, 'He's recording everything!'"

Nate shrugs. He says, "Real Maine People."

He's explaining what has just transpired, and I like what he's said, I think, because there's a kind of truth in it and not just the truth of Nate being Nate. At the same time, though, what Nate has said is implicitly exclusionary, suggesting that if you do not behave as, for example, some people sometimes behave in the office of The Wood Mill of Maine, then you are not a *real* Mainer. (Superiority is always implicit in exclusion.) In addition, this kind of categorizing can too easily be exculpatory, a plea of innocence, a way to dismiss individual agency and responsibility. You can't help yourself because this is how Real Mainers behave—that kind of thing. The boys are just being boys. Nate is just being Nate. I am just being I. But, see, even as I write those words now, I realize that I am contradicting myself. But I also think that I am not contradicting myself.

No, I know what you mean, I think Nate would say.

But do you know what I mean? I can hear him asking.

And I do know what he means and I don't think he's wrong, but I think I'm right also.

Bjarki says, "They're saying Texas might go to Biden. All these California liberals moved there and want to make Texas like California, and that's *after* they fucked California so bad they can't live there anymore."

The wildfires in California this year—augmented by climate change—have again been the worst on record, more than four million acres burned, an area a fifth the size of Maine. It will be worse next year. To prevent its immolation, the most massive tree on the planet, a giant sequoia "named" for a Civil War general, will be wrapped in protective foil.

"Now we got all these Massholes and New Yorkers coming up to Maine."

Have I not mentioned that Bjarki is not a U.S. citizen? In fact, he's a German and Icelandic citizen, a green card holder, paying taxes but not permitted to vote. He says, "It ain't natural. It ain't normal. When I moved up here, *I* didn't come looking to fucking change Mercer. I just wanted the lifestyle of being left alone. And I was an outsider from day one. If you're not from Maine, you're a flatlander. Aw man, you know what they're like. Flatlanders want things now now now. They aren't used to pouring coffee at the gas station. They're like, 'Hi, I'd like a blahblahblah,' like Starbucks. And Christy's is like, 'Get fucked. We're not serving you Massholes coffee.'"

The license plates read VACATIONLAND.

The big green road signs say THE WAY LIFE SHOULD BE.

THE PINE TREE STATE.

GET AWAY FROM IT ALL.

"You can't get there from here."

"I went to the woods because I wished to live deliberately, to front only the essential facts of life, and see if I could learn what it had to teach, and not, when I came to die, discover that I had not lived. . . . I wanted to live deep and suck out all the marrow of life, to live so sturdily and Spartan-like as to put to rout all that was not life, to cut a broad swath and shave close, to drive life into a corner and reduce it to its lowest terms, and, if it proved to be mean, why then to get the whole and genuine meanness of it and publish its meanness to the world."

"When they took his leg off—my brother, E, he has obesity, diabetes, dementia, fucking everything. He orders all his food online and it's nothing but sugar. Aww, he's addicted. Oreos. Honey Buns. They took his leg to the knee. And they warned us—'He will go through some emotional issues.' Well, yesterday he left a message, 'Mykael, they're holding me hostage—' You know, he's shitting himself and he won't let any nurses near him. He thinks there's a conspiracy—"

The phone rings.

"—that we are all conspiring—"

"Good morning, The Wood Mill."

"—and he goes, 'When I get out of this place, I'm going fucking up in the woods and build me a cabin and nobody's going to know where I am.' He's slurring his words. 'Mykael, I don't want to hear from none of you, ever again.' And I'm like, 'Okay, Peg Leg!'"

Nate says I need a cat. I tell Nate I have a cat, but that the cat is at Robinson Street, with B. We've been separated for some time now. Over the past week, I've been living in a small camp deep in the woods of Rome. I'll be spending a lot of time there this summer and fall, doing repairs and renovations, right up on the edge of the lake that Bjarki and Myke and I ice fished three years ago, just down a hill from where the North Pond Hermit lived for twenty-six years.

"I lost my identity," Christopher Knight said. "There was no audience, no one to perform for. To put it romantically, I was completely free."

Each day, as the camp warms, the smell of rodents rises. In the night, I awake to pattering in the attic, scratching behind my pillow, something somebody once told me.

There are now a half dozen Victor spring-loaded traps in my truck.

On the phone, Bjarki says, "Nothing's guaranteed in life. A buddy just showed up with some boards that are completed rotted."

I hear the word *buddy* and pretend not to hear it.

The night before Election Day, we eat behind Thai Smile, in the Sequoia, which is either Bjarki's or Bjarki's mom's or Bjarki's family's SUV and which I have taken to occasionally referring to as The Tree. The last time I saw Bjarki was when he'd visited me in Rome. "You *are* in the middle of nowhere," he said when he arrived. Then he helped me lift a picture window into place and refused compensation. In the lake, the sky and the clouds were the soft grays and lavenders of winter, contrasting sharply with the oranges and golds of maple and beech, bright bursts of color that seemed to be expanding in my periphery, thrown to me like a flower.

"It's pretty," Bjarki said.

He pointed to the shore where he used to walk with Rylee.

Mercer, he said, was starting to feel crowded and claustrophobic. He was looking into buying a remote stretch of land farther north, near Moosehead Lake. He imagined posting KEEP THE FUCK OUT signs around the property.

"And you'll still be wicked tight with your neighbors." I wasn't kidding.

"It's so pretty," he said.

In the camp's kitchen, the gas lights *poof*ed as I lit them, shining, it seemed, like a realization upon a pile of paper—notes and transcripts—which I quickly set aside. My iPhone wasn't recording that night because sometimes I just wanted to hang out without The Book in the background, which of course was impossible. The Book was everywhere. I mean, even though the walls and the roof and the floor of the camp were pine, and the table was pine, and the cabinets and the countertops were pine, and it sort of felt like you were inside a giant pine tree, which would have been a perfect setting for The Book, that night with Bjarki, I just wanted the two of us to be a couple of meaningless dudes hanging with a couple of meaningless cans of beer, and I suppose we sort of were. We talked a lot about the North Pond Hermit that night, just as we are talking about him now, with our Thai food in The Tree.

Bjarki says, "I want to know why? What made him want to leave society?"

He suggests I write to Christopher Knight. "Maybe mention that you're writing a book, but if you tell him you're writing about The Wood Mill, he'll be like, 'Never heard of it. Don't care. Fuck off.' So maybe don't tell him that the book isn't about *him*, but kind of tell him, 'Hey, I'm genuinely interested in you because I'm fixing the camp where you used to live.' Maybe he'd. . . . How do you pick someone's brain and get them to sign up for something like that?"

Bjarki says, "Nate, I got some bad news."

"What you got?"

"Matthew's floor cupped."

"Who's Matthew?"

I say, "This guy."

Nate says, "I was like, '*Which one? There's a lot of Matthews!*'"

(Soon after I arrived in Florida, before the snow really started to fall in Maine, B sent me several photos of the dead birds and rodents that our cat had brought in through the cat door. It didn't have anything to do with me and B, not really. We were both proud of the cat, our own little murderer, and disgusted, the murderer. It was amazing, how precise she was, and clean. No kidding. Though The Wood Mill of Maine floor may have refused me, it has always been quite stunning with the morning sun angling across all those thousands of years, all that history, that little pile of intestines, that small kidney, those feathers. Some of my friends say that house cats are decimating songbird populations and I don't disagree. Still, I tell them that our cat never once brought in a robin. Climate change, I say. Habitat loss, pesticides, cars, fucking skyscrapers. I was trying to meditate down there. To separate or not to separate, that was the question. But I got distracted. That old banyan marking the entrance to J's condo—its trunk was filled with bees. At first it pissed me off that someone had sprayed foam into the tree's trunk, to keep the bees out, but then I saw that the bees had outmaneuvered the foam and were coming and going freely, whizzing past of their own accord, not like thoughts at all. I am as grandiose as any Happy Meal. I really am. To assign meaning is an awful power. Once, B asked me, totally serious, totally out of the blue, "Is life-saving hyphenated?" It was me who killed Beauty, her big leafy plant. She froze to death in the back of the U-Haul as I drove from Wyoming to Maine. For a while we saw a therapist and I got some pills that made things easier for me and she started taking her temperature and we scheduled times and then one day she told me. I never know what to say. During one of our phone calls, I remember she said that the smoke detector at Robinson Street had been chirping for several weeks. I do not believe that science understands fire. The alarm that signaled the end of my sitting meditations kept a violent, mercurial time. I was always running out of gin. I liked to sit with a frosted glass in this overstuffed chair that was probably more accurately described as a loveseat. No kidding, I was watching all these cinema vérité documentaries down there, films where there's no obvious plot or protagonist and the whole movie is just a bunch of scenes. No soundtrack, no interviews, no reenactments. The deceptions are so blatant; it's audacious. In one Frederick Wiseman film, *Belfast, Maine* (1999), a community theatre performer says, "You can't eat the orange and throw the peel away—a man is not a piece of fruit! Now pay attention!"

I tell you, I did too. I turned my head all the way around.

Belfast is about ninety minutes up the coast from Robinson Street. You are following just behind a man carrying a bucket through a low, wet morning. Off-screen, a dog *woofs*. What is in the bucket?

The dog, in sight now, whirls at the end of a chain. The dog is a coyote. The coyote fills the screen. Gray-green eyes, tail tipped black, raised hackles, the life of it.

A single echoing shot.

I tell you, I couldn't sleep. The virus was everywhere down there. I lay in my little bed listening to the helicopters over the golf course, the multitudes at the door, my own panting.)

SEVENTEEN

Shavings (Lovejoy)

A twenty-incher approaches the Pinheiro. There are knots in this board, but so what. There are no knots I can't disappear.

Hunter sneezes.

"Bless you!"

The twenty-inch board stops. The conveyor has also stopped. Nate removes his Puma hat, scratches his head, turns off the planer. He moves around the infeed table abruptly, delicately, a songbird in your hedge.

The Board is so wide and beautiful there, before it enters the future.

On, off. On, off. *Psst, psst.*

The infeed table throbs, conveying nothing.

"Come on!"

Hunter stands by.

Hunter runs for hydraulic fluid.

"Ah! Son of a fuck!"

"That whole thing's got to come out?"

That whole thing is a Lovejoy coupling, a mechanical connection that has something to do with transmitting rotational torque in The Book.

Nate hammers the broken Lovejoy with a sledge and a screwdriver.

Replacing it is no big deal, you know what I mean; it breaks every few years so I've got an extra on hand but to take this one out and replace it—we won't be running any twenties till tomorrow.

But I only have today.

"You know, depending on who you talk to, a twenty-inch clear—some people are like, 'Those don't exist.' Turn that wheel for me."

Hunter turns the infeed roller.

"Riding along in my automobile," sing Chuck Berry and Nate and Hunter and me.

"Faster."

"Anxious to tell the way I feel."

"Faster."

"No particular place to go."

EIGHTEEN

Shavings (*Laccaria*)

I *finally* own up to the big lie I've been telling myself—one of them any-way—in the summer of 2020, about six months before the U.S. Capitol is overtaken by a mob. We are in The Tree, towing The Wood Mill's Club Cadet to a mechanic. Actually, Bjarki says, the UTV is a *Cub* Cadet, not a *Club*.

Bjarki juts his hand out the window to signal a left turn.

The trailer's blinkers and brake lights don't work.

"These fucking truck drivers, man—they're *wildly* unprofessional when it comes to not rear-ending people."

I hadn't known that about truck drivers. A tractor trailer is behind us.

We turn onto a dirt road, a wall of corn on either side. The broad green leaves are covered in dust. Further on, through a stand of trees, we glimpse the skin of people and the Sandy River splashing. Some people say that you can't step into the same river twice, but they're just showing off. There is only the one river. You just go ahead and try to step out of it.

Bjarki says, "One of my straps didn't hold."

The chartreuse strap flaps behind us. These days, Bjarki often seems older than he did back in 2017, which I guess makes sense, and also doesn't.

The road bends sharply. We are now approximately paralleling the Kennebec River, where, almost three hundred years ago, in 1724, a party of British colonists ambushed and burned a Norridgewock (Narantsouack) village. Dozens of villagers were killed. Those attempting to swim to safety were shot. The brown river turned red. Flames ate the sky. Scalps were carried to Boston. Though it is unclear exactly how much was paid for the scalps of the villagers, it was likely less than the one hundred pounds paid for the scalp of a Jesuit priest.

Forest borders both sides of the road now. Houses are set in small, tidy clearings. A blue tarp covers a roof. Tomato plants in pots. Toy vehicles. Wood piles. A fully armed Rambo wearing Donald Trump's face. The repair shop is a garage beside a modular home. Inside the dark space, a man sits on a bucket, addressing a small tire. He is smoking. A radio plays.

Bjarki has typed and printed a list of repairs. He says, "The windshield wiper keeps falling off." He says "CV boots" and "compression rods" and "radiator fan." He offers a business card. "It's a crazy name, so, um, good luck."

"Say it to me."

Bjarki says, "Bjarki."

We drive away through a rolling green hayfield. Bjarki points to a spindly red machine in the field.

He says, "That's a hay tedder."

Though I have no idea what a hay tedder is, I know there is no such thing as a *random* hay tedder. I'm thinking about a time when I asked Bjarki about accidents and injuries at The Wood Mill and he said, "This didn't happen at *my* mill, but it was on the exact same kind of planer that we have. A guy got scalped. He had a ponytail and his hair got sucked in and the planer ripped the hair—the whole—just scalped him. He died, you know. He didn't live. At least, I think he died. Nate knows more about it than I do."

Nate said, "Something like that *could* have happened." He said, "Let's see if I can word it correctly. I don't know if Bjarki embellishes what he hears or. . . . Sometimes, I'll be like, 'Dude that's not true at all,' and he'll be like, 'Yeah it is,' and I'll be like, 'No. It's not.' He doesn't mean anything. He's just telling a story."

A hay tedder flips cut hay to facilitate its drying.

"It's so funny, Bjarki, when I started writing that magazine-style essay—I don't know—I was like, 'The Wood Mill of Maine is this badass company that sells these badass boards.' But you maybe only do one floor of twenty-inchers a year."

"Three or four probably."

"So have you received those orders yet this year?"

"Ahh, nope."

And while it's true that Bjarki and Nate never explicitly said that The Wood Mill of Maine sells *a ton* of twenty-inch-wide pine floors, they have obviously sold *some*. I've held those boards. I've felt their heft, hooked them with a diamond jig, swallowed them uncooked and whole. The human brain is a wondrous understatement. Tell me where I can find consciousness. I'd like to go there, and touch it. I have recently dreamt of an Indian who breaks down my door. He may or may not be there to reveal how my unconscious is filled only with old tropes. His head is as large as a five-gallon bucket. It is either happening a long time ago or a long time in the future or it is happening right now. The cabin's floor is dirt. The man grabs my belt to throw me somewhere. Of course everything means *something*. It means *everything*. I mean, there's probably some kind of highbrow argument to be made about how, as floors changed from dirt to straw to stone to wood to Pergo—*evolved*, some might say—mankind grew to feel superior to and then separate from the Earth. But what is not the Earth? Of course I am mankind. Of course I understand that getting to know someone is not a joke for a book, not a joke at all, while at the same time, I also know that I am the world's biggest joke. I think I fancy getting myself a Facebook page. I want followers. I crave likes. Somebody, please, DM me the meaning of an eggplant. Nate, Nate, Nate, I've got some bad news. All belief is creative, in the generative sense. By believing in something, I create that thing. I make it real. I make reality—a *new* reality, that is—one that possesses all the potency of truth. We know this, and yet, believe me, we are also so adept at forgetting. Knock, knock. Would you rather someone pay more or less to possess the hair on your head? To possess you? Do not think that I am trying to absolve anyone of anything. I'm just saying, "The ice cream place is along here someplace," Bjarki says. He says most of the orders The Wood Mill of Maine takes for twenty-inch-wide boards are not composed *exclusively* of twenties. Mostly, those widest boards are mixed in with other widths, and mostly, the twenties people order *aren't* the knotless boards I'm writing about, which means, it seems, that the only pure floor that The Wood Mill manufactures is the floor in my mind, obviously—I guess—which means that I have been writing all this time about something that is emphatically *not* The Wood Mill of Maine, which raises the question: What *is* The Wood Mill of Maine?

Metaphorically, this is easy enough.

But literally?—*Literally*, Bjarki and I are stepping from The Tree onto dazzling blacktop. An unmasked man asks if we are looking for a haircut. Imagine *looking for a haircut*! In the shadow of the gas station, the red, white, and blue of a barber's pole go up and up and up, without going up at all. There is no ice cream here. We climb back into The Tree. This July will be the hottest in

Maine's recorded history. It is discomfiting to know that I am contributing to the setting of so many records that I'd prefer went unset, but at the same time, what is one to do? For every gallon of gasoline that burns, or combusts, or explodes, or whatever it is that happens under the Sequoia's hood, we travel between thirteen and seventeen miles. It's called Frederick's. Here, the mint chocolate chip is the green kind. Bjarki orders "hard chocolate" in a waffle cone, but they are out of waffle cones, so he gets a sugar cone.

We lick.

We taste.

We swallow.

We carry the boards into Robinson Street together, splitting the weight of each stack against our hips or across our shoulders—a kind of bridge between us—two men working, talking a little, a little shyly, and all the while, I remember, I admire each board's specific nuance and grace. The lighter sapwood! The darker pith! The small black knots set like rocks in a stream, spooling and spinning the annual growth rings about them and from them. Board upon board upon board we carry them, the trace of pine dust soft as we carry them, our noses twitching back sneezes, sweat stinging our eyes and falling in drops, becoming on the boards' faces circles vibrant with contrast and color and definition, illuminated as if by a magnifying glass trained to a previously unfocused spot on a page.

How I'd like to speak with that young man now—me, I mean—to hold him.

It wasn't the boards' fault. Or The Wood Mill's. Or the fasteners'. Or Nate's or Bjarki's or mine, not really, not exclusively. Because I'd insisted on laying the floor as tightly as possible, taking special care to eliminate all the gaps and separations, when the pine's Matthew Clark (MC) increased and the floor began to grow, the edges of each board had nowhere to go but up. Nowhere. Not ever. Suddenly we were drinking out of cups. (Sponges, straws, bottles, bulldozers.) In several places, the cupping was so pronounced that you'd be walking along gracefully and—*wham!*—a foot ambush. It was like something that had been foretold, something out of Aesop, both metaphorical and hysterical, like everything, I guess. It's funny, though, my obsession with gaplessness is, apparently, highly particular, because the original one-hundred-and-seventy-year-old boards that remain on the second floor at Robinson

Street have gaps a mile wide, and *those* gaps don't bother me at all. In addition, those original floorboards are spruce, *not* pine, as I may have earlier led you to believe. (The *sub*floors at Robinson Street are pine. And the sheathing, and some of the framing.) I suppose you could say that all deception creates separation—from yourself maybe, or truth, or The World—a gap filled with old rags and the husks of ladybugs and needles and nothing. But I suppose you could also say that nothing is not a deception—that there is only separation. By moving in and living upon that choppy sea of pine, by not *doing* anything to fix the floor, by proceeding as if nothing had happened, I mean, it *was* as if nothing had happened. Except that something *had* happened.

"So she moved out?"

"Yeah."

"You single?"

"Married, but *separated*."

"I'm sorry. I didn't think—"

"Communication, bro," I say. "Communication." In retrospect, I wish I hadn't said *bro. Bro* didn't really feel like me, though it must have been. And what the hell is communication anyway?

We are back at the office now, just the two of us.

Bjarki says, "I've been basically single for eight years. You can do whatever the fuck you want and you don't need to report to nobody."

The phone rings.

"Excuse me," he says.

When he hangs up, I say, "I don't *think* I want to be single for the rest of my life, but I don't really know."

Bjarki nods. He recounts the trauma and possibility of the dating world— *the dating world!* He's trying to cheer me up.

"Shit," he says. "I got to hit the road."

But then he doesn't hit the road. He asks about The Book and I talk about the process of transcribing voice memos and he says, "I don't like talking about myself."

That's like me too.

He says, "Anyone who talks about themself always ends up sounding like an asshole."

"I'm not trying to make you sound like an asshole."

"I know."

But I'm not sure that he does know. Or really, I'm not sure that *I know* what I'm trying to make Bjarki sound like, or look like—besides *him*, or *me*, whatever *we are*—and so, in an attempt to reassure us both, I say probably way too much about the everyday heroics of an eggplant.

I'm serious. There is so much courage in the morning. The sincerity of my feelings on this point rains from my eyeballs. ("So what are we gonna do today?"

"You're going to put boards away."

"Which boards?"

"The twelve-inch boards." (Board upon board upon board they carry them.)) I'm leaning against the pine counter and leaning back from the pine counter. I mean, I definitely *don't* want to make Bjarki look like an asshole. I don't think he is an asshole. He *isn't*. But at the same time, I know how easy it is to make anyone look ridiculous. Everyone *is* ridiculous. Although, of course, I'm not saying that all assholes are *necessarily* ridiculous. All assholes are beautiful. That is, all assholes are beautiful except for me, for I am quite exceptional, unlike the rest of you beautiful world-betterers. I am the asshole within the asshole, the most superior, the best asshole. It's dark in here and not funny. I suppose I had thought that my book—The Book—by making the world a better place, would allow me to escape from the asshole's asshole and achieve goodness and worth. It was my own little hero's journey. (Outmoded, says J.) Of course, it was also an impossible project, I knew that, just like Robinson Street. That's why I'd dreamt it up. Dear Hemingway, I have never written one true sentence. But if we are not here to make the world a better place, then I do not know why we are here. And yet, I am quite certain *why*, and yet, I do not care *why*, and yet, there is nothing more important than *why*, and yet, there is no *why*, and yet, there are more *why*s than I can dream, and yet, one plus one does equal one and I love ice cream and who's fault is that? They say that objects in the mirror are closer than they appear, but in fact, those objects could not be farther away. Forgive me, World, for though I know that I am a part of you, I also feel so far apart. One of the greatest sadnesses I have known is my inability to love you constantly. Us constantly. Forget the ticks and the senators, the noose and the scalpel, even the deceiver, *Laccaria*, and the clarinet, and the calm and smashing oceans I have met with indifference. The miscarriage occurred in spring, early in the term. The sounds of pain came first. Then there were phone calls. There was ibuprofen. For some time, there was the absence of sound. Then I heard a body moving. I heard the toilet. Later, I saw spots on the floor. Later, we did not speak of it. Perhaps we have never spoken of anything. What, for heaven's sake, have I done to my liver? I must eat less bacon, use shampoo and a loofah, get serious. My therapist, after each of our sessions, she sterilizes her office with bleach, Our Fathers, and fumigation. A polished stone hangs from her neck. I'm telling you, I'm her most interesting and incurable patient, superior to all the rest. In fact, I'm so pathologically good at being me, she's writing a whole book on the subject so that after you finish my book, you might actually figure out the real honest-to-god rangoon about us all.

NINETEEN

Shavings (Rangoon III (Unrealization))

Election Day morning dawns cold and snowy. In the office, I'm barely awake after a night spent on Bjarki's couch fending off both the attacks of his two kittens and the dehydrating effects of his woodstove, which had just *cheeched* right along, Bjarki said, pumping out the *bitoos*, Bjarki said, hot enough to set the pitch in pine, I thought, and, as it happened, pull the secret from me—the water, that is—so that now my head feels as if it is repelling an atmosphere of lead. I take long drinks from a gallon jug. The label indicates water from Poland Spring, but in reality the water is from Bjarki's tap. But where is the *real* in reality? Where is the real *in reality*? Across the yard, snow slowly melts from the pole barn's metal roof.

"All right," I say, "I should probably go put this door in."

Ahead of me on Route 2, a slow-moving plow sends pebbles of salt bounding over the road as playfully as cats. I have never before seen cats in salt, never seen so many cats on the road, run over so many cats. Jesus. Or whomever. Maybe the kittens wouldn't have used the word *attack*. Dirt shoulder white with snow. I'm pretty happy going slow. I'll be working on the north side of the camp in Rome today, the lake side. There will be wind off the water— the north wind—and the sun will never reach me. I know this well enough. What else? Don't forget the jigsaw for the cat door. The radio in the truck intermittently and unpredictably loses the signal I think is what is happening. TRUMP. TRUMP. The old Grange hall. The Sticky Diamond THC and marijuana shop. Chain-link fence. Chained dog barking. I turn down the camp's narrow dirt road, tunneling through a mixed hardwood and hemlock forest. Hemlock is never mentioned by the earliest colonial observers. That is, those colonial observers either could not see the hemlock or did not see that it was not spruce or fir or pine, all of which they catalogued extensively. In patches of snow, I see a single set of four-wheeler tracks. I have read that the hemlock woolly adelgid is making its way north and east, killing trees. The only unfallen leaves now are the oak and the beech—brown and beige and yellow. The man standing beside the four-wheeler isn't tall, but he's padded out with a combination of orange and camouflage and jowl, blue jeans and boots. The gun is holstered on his right side. He's checking his traps, he says, indicating a tan-and-gray coyote. The man's teeth are big, his gums red. The coyote looks so small, so still, so dead, lying on the ground swept clean of snow and leaves by her struggle. In fact, the man says, she is not dead—not *yet*, he says—despite the two bullets in her head.

The pistol is a .22, a revolver. Though I'm not sure he's placed it there, I feel the man's hand atop the truck's cab. He makes a joke that has something to do with trapping animals and pornography and, because I want to seem as if I understand, I grin maniacally. Then I roll up the window, turn on the heat, bump and squeak.

Clouds rush over the serrated lake. The light turns silver then gray. It begins to snow, stops snowing, snows some more. The door goes in about as easily as one might expect, except that I have forgotten to order a door-knob. *Jigsaw*. I drive through the dimming afternoon, eating the remnants of my cold lunch. *Home Despot* some people call it. Under the bright lights of the box store, everyone is wearing masks. Back at The Wood Mill, Bjarki is browsing forklifts online. The fate of the world remains unknown.

"The UPS guy was in. He's like, 'I need answers!'"

Though I am sorry to have missed the UPS guy this afternoon, he *had* been in the office the day before.

The day before, the UPS guy says, "What's up with this time change?"

"Only a Democrat would cut a foot off the bottom of a blanket and sew it to the top to make a longer blanket."

"We're screwed either way. They're either going to riot or shut the economy down."

"If Trump loses, you know he's gonna fuck shit up for his last three months."

The UPS guy says, "I don't think he's vindictive. I just laugh. It's like LePage. Everybody got all horned-up over whatever he said, but he didn't try to candy-coat it. It's like, if you can't handle the truth—"

A few minutes later, after the UPS guy leaves, Bjarki and I climb into The Tree.

"Holy fucking dark and it's only four forty-five!"

The clock in the dash reads 6:26.

Bjarki says the blue time is off by a daylight saving hour. It's actually 5:26. We pass a Dollar General that was not there the month before. A Dunkin' is going in next door. When we get to Thai Smile, Bjarki orders the Dragon Roll without looking at the menu and I look at the menu and order a spicy tuna roll and when I offer to pay, Bjarki pays. He says, "Look at it this way, The Book's going to be a huge amount of advertising for The Wood Mill. Someone's going to call and say, 'I read this book and I need that twenty-inch-wide floor!'"

We carry the plastic bags to the parking lot.

Bjarki says, "My house is a mess."

"Okay."

"I don't know what I'm going to do."

"All right."

"It's bad."

Bjarki turns on the heat in The Tree. He says, "In eighth grade, we learned about Henry David Thoreau. His statement was like, *I came into the woods to leave society, to find a life of whatever whatever.* Half the kids were like, 'He's a crazy old man.' And I was just. . . . 'No, no, this makes perfect sense.' Some judge was like, 'By being born into this society, you agree to the terms and conditions.' And he's like, 'Well, fuck you. I don't wanna. I'm gonna go live *alone.* Like, 'I'll go fuckin' *not* be part of society.'"

We eat our food, then Bjarki backs us out of the rye.

A nearly full moon is rising.

Loudly, like B and I used to say, I say, "Moon!"

Bjarki says that yesterday the moon was blue.

The word *lunatic* comes from *lunar,* and *loony* may come from both the satellite and the bird. Sometimes, as a result of particles in the atmosphere, like after a forest fire or a volcanic eruption, the moon *will appear* tinted blue, but that's not what Bjarki means. As far as I can tell, the first written occurrence of *blue moon* came from a 1528 dialogue:

O church men are wyly foxes
More crafty then juggelers boxes . . .

Yf they saye the mone is belewe
We must believe that it is true

We are going sixty miles an hour through the dark and then we pull into
Bjarki's driveway and argue intensely about the Paris Climate Accords and
labor unions and the EPA, trying to solve the world's problems—to make
the world a better place. As I come around the side of The Tree, Bjarki is
waving his arms at the motion sensors on his house. Apparently, they can't
sense us. Footsteps sound hollowly on dark frozen deck boards. The glass
door slides open and shut. The kittens scatter. The power is out.

Bjarki says, "I really wanted to vacuum."

And then, as if on cue, the lights come on. There are clothes piled on the
couch and Bjarki folds them. He vacuums. We get that fire a-*cheeching* and
then, now, the next night, the night of Election Day, we arrive at Bjarki's house
and turn on the lights and Bjarki, sweeping up Mr. Crowley, says, "Hey kitty,
Matty's going to install your door. What do you think of that?"

The door at the back of Bjarki's utility room opens to the garage. In pencil,
on the door's lower left panel, Bjarki has traced an outline of the cat door:
a *U* with a flat top.

I say, "Here we go, bub."

And then I put in the cat door.

This is true. And also not true.

First, what I did was drill four holes in Bjarki's outline.

"Hold on a second," he said. "You skipped step one."

He held out a can of Budweiser to me and he opened one too and we
both took big swigs and in that moment, I felt myself to be happy. Then I lay
on my side and addressed the door. The TV was not on. Though the blade
in the jigsaw wasn't meant for metal, I had thought it would work okay on
the metal-clad door, and though it did work, it worked worse than okay. I
changed the blade. Bjarki was watching me. I wanted badly for everything in
my performance to appear planned and efficient and competent. Supposedly,
I was a carpenter doing carpentry. Supposedly, I was a writer writing a book.
Supposedly, I was me being me. Bits of foam from the door's core scattered
across the floor. When I finally got the *U* cut out, it was of course too small.

I said, "I always do this. I do this with everything."

"You like things tight," he said.

"I make everything too tight," I said.

Bjarki offered me the Sawzall. He said, "Locked and loaded."

I had been afraid the Sawzall would be too aggressive, but it worked fine. *Phwap. Phwap.* Now the cats can access the garage, though not the outdoors. I turn off my Voice Memos app, which had, apparently, recorded all of this. Large mostly white people on the widescreen television are telling us things. ABC. FOX. ABC. FOX. I slide open the glass door and step onto the porch to cool off with the moon and when I come back, Cat Stevens runs out through my legs. "Hey!" Bjarki knifes past. He's bent stiffly at the waist, both arms outstretched toward what they are not holding, the cat, which is all arches and leaping grace. In shadow, Bjarki's wooden jerks play smoothly across the snow, the forms of the two creatures lengthening, overlapping, turning in impossible ways. Even the longest moment is already past. Bjarki lunges, snatches the animal, and returns to the house murmuring love and reprimands. We drink several more beers. At some point, I receive a text message that reads, *DOOM.* Or maybe I send that text. *Phwap, phwap.* "They figured it out! Dude, they figured it out!" Bjarki sets a 9 mm handgun on the table next to the beer cans and an unopened bottle of Bird Dog Whiskey and takes a picture.

"Election night in Maine."

When Texas goes for Trump, we decide to go to bed.

I say, "What if I do something and we both wake up dead?"

Bjarki looks amused, perplexed. He takes the gun into the bedroom with him. I had always thought that shooting guns with Bjarki would be symbolic of something or other, but maybe *not*-shooting guns is also symbolic. I lie on the couch with my head away from the stove. The snow in the yard is blue in the moonlight. The blue is the snow in your mind. The mountains had burned that summer, but the sky was clear, bluer than anything. B's mother had made the dress. I don't know why but I had it in my mind that it was a bad omen to see your bride's dress before she was in it and then I saw the dress hanging in the window and I immediately wished that I had not seen it and when I told B, she said it didn't matter. Every dream is real until you wake up. The night before, as Bjarki and I sat waiting for our food, when he'd suggested that The Book would be great advertising for The Wood Mill, I didn't tell him that there probably weren't going to be many twenty-inch boards in The Book. What I said was that The Book was going to be published in Europe, which wasn't a lie exactly, but was pretty ridiculous, considering that I didn't even know if The Book was going to be published at all, if it was ever going to be a book—whatever that is.

He said, "I remember when you first started, it was just going to be a—"

"A magazine-style essay," I said. I said, "Now there's all kinds of stuff going on."

And that's when Bjarki said it, the exact words I'd planned to say myself—to write, I mean, in The Book.

Let me guess, he said, "I am the eastern white pine."

In fact though, it *wasn't* exactly what I'd planned to write, for though the words were exactly the words I had intended to write, the sentiment as Bjarki expressed it was *not* at all what I had intended, not at all what I had thought The Book was building toward, like its cathartic core or whatever. You see, my hope had always been that my words, *his* words, *those* words would carry or deliver or possess, or whatever words do or are or have, some gravitas—*gravitas!*—which would then elicit in the reader a deep feeling of unity with the pine tree, which would then elicit a deep connection with all trees and then also Bjarki and me and B and all the people in the world and The World itself—the whole mystical enchilada, I mean—and then, that *oneness*, that feeling of total connection, I mean, would inarguably serve to make the world a better place. Imagine a mystical enchilada in a Thai restaurant in central Maine. That was my hope. And The Book wasn't even *about* pine trees, not really. Plus, the manner in which Bjarki said what he said was so *blasé*, which—*blasé*—was a word I planned to never use again. Or maybe it was just too *wry*. Or both. Or something else. I didn't really know what either of those words meant, not really, not exactly. You see, for the whole pine tree thing to work, I'd always figured it had to be an emphatic and joyful *yawp* in the style of Whitman (*I too am not a bit tamed, I too am untranslatable*), not Bjarki's bored acknowledgment, spoken as if those words in that specific order at this particular point in the fiery (and icy) expansion of the universe had somehow become so thoroughly commercialized and trite and hackneyed that they didn't *mean* anything and that—and this was the worst part—*of course* he was the eastern white pine. He had known it all along. It was I—*I!*—who hadn't already realized this obvious fact, so that in that moment, as Bjarki failed to fully realize my big intended realization for him as I imagined it being realized in The Book, he was actually realizing something else. Or I was, or *am*. Bjarki was realization personified, if that's not too much. I mean, *he* was—he *is* the realization. His attitude, his expression, his posture—his original unmasked face without a mask and my original unmasked face with a mask and the soft music that I think is Thai music and the chairs that I think are chairs—all of it prompted the realization that the supposedly great realization of The Book had all already been realized before and also, I felt, written, and I didn't want to write what had already been written, by Whitman or anyone else, though I wouldn't have minded writing some of the good stuff *before* Walt wrote it. My friend J, he says that The World, I'm quoting him now—exists in the gaps between us. I like the expansiveness of this proposition, but on the one hand, it suggests that if there are no gaps, there is no World. Or maybe it suggests there are only gaps and only World. What time is it? I mean, in my overheated blue-snow half sleep, I am either remembering something I have realized before or realizing it for the first time, that all of life—whatever that is—can be viewed as an infinite sequence of realizations and that each of these realizations is also an infinitude of failed realizations and that all of these realized and unrealized realizations can be boiled down into two categories: realizations of connection and realizations of separation—as if realizations can be *boiled*. (But why can't they be boiled?) And then I'm thinking that at least on some level, to actually feel separate, you must also actually feel connected, for how can you be separate from something that you are not already connected to? And how can you connect to something that you are not already separate from? I want to say that I saw pine needles sprouting from Bjarki's eyebrows, but I did not. And I want to say that I felt my roots tap through the building's foundation, but I did not. I realized that I was hungry, that realizing itself was like knowing—*is* knowing—and that both knowing and realizing are actually both a connection *and* a separation and can not only be one or the other thing and so in wanting to connect with Bjarki and The World, I must also want to be separate from them. The Book, I'm thinking, is not a project in connection alone, but a project in separation *and* connection. A door within a door. *Phwap. Phwap.* But what *good* does realization do? Does the moon shine brighter? Has the war stopped? Do I love you more? I have had panic attacks before. I remember the darkroom of one particular photography class in college. I'd eaten a pot brownie beforehand, and then, when I felt that I wasn't feeling the drugs, I ate another brownie and then another and then I skipped off to class—*Happy as a lark,* as B would say. In that small black space with the red lights and the red-lit faces, I freaked out. I mean, I *freaked* out. I was at that time writing a term paper relating some Buddhist concept or other to Walt Whitman's *Song of Myself,* which somehow helps me to understand how I have come to be here now, how *we* have come to be here now, or *then,* a couple of pine trees in a Thai place quoting poetry. And what I shall assume you shall assume, for every knot belonging to me as good belongs to you. *Phwap. Phwap.* I don't mean to be hyperbolic, but when I finally eased my circular saw screaming into the floor, of course it had nothing to do with me and B. Oh say can you see. DeWalt. I went straight to what I thought was the heart of the matter, the very center of the first floor, where two floorboards met in the most treacherous cup, a kind of wooden standing wave where the incoming tide collides with the river coursing out. The saw wailed. The shavings flew. And then everything stopped. The saw wouldn't start and the saw wouldn't budge. Nor could I lift the tool from the floor. The blade itself was stuck—trapped by The Wood Mill of Maine. So many times in my life I have not known why, but this kind of bind was familiar to me, one that I'd encountered before, albeit mostly in the vertical, in load-bearing timbers, when the pressure on a cutting blade is created by gravity and mass. In this case, the floor at Robinson Street was exerting such an expansive force that even as I cut out a saw blade's width of pine—a kerf—the floor, like brake pads on a bike rim, closed this gap so tightly that the spinning blade ceased to spin. There wasn't any water that I could see, but it was clearly there, the secret, doing secret things. Thank you, water. Thank you, before. Thank you, after. Now I sat with my hands on my knees looking at myself reflected in the floor, seeing myself in the floor, not so much the whiskery scruff of me but a shadow I both recognized and didn't spanning the blue chalk line that I'd snapped and the yellow-and-black saw and I saw the tree's years in the wood too, in or under my shadow, and after a minute like that, doing whatever it was you'd say I was doing, or being, I abruptly got to my feet and retrieved some wedges and a pry bar and a hammer. Eventually, I removed two three-inch-wide strips of floor, one by the bathroom and one by the pantry. Underneath these floorboards you'll find what you find. I'd found the name of the carpenter who built the house on Robinson Street penciled in a graceful script on the back of a piece of window trim—*J. C. Harris*, a one-hundred-seventy-year-old signature—and I eventually planned to do something with that board, I just didn't know what. (I had also found *living* penciled on a piece of trim in the living room.) The patches I fashioned from old pine I'd salvaged from somewhere else in the house and though I sanded them flat and smooth, for whatever reason—laziness, probably—I never finished them with any oil or wax or poly-whatever. Now these two darker stripes—without gloss, gloss-less—look a little out of place. It's funny, though, I kind of like how the lizard tells a story while the rest of the floor ripples like a song. Cat Stevens, left foot, Mr. Crowley, right foot. Of course it will all seem like apophenia to someone else. Of course all mirrors are liars. Whitman was a Gemini. In the morning, I wake up, and then I hear Bjarki wake up and still we don't know anything. We are awake now and we know nothing. I fill my gallon jug from the tap and we get our coffee from Christy's and then, in The Wood Mill of Maine's office, we all say *Non!* in caricatured French and as I leave to go put a knob in a door in Rome, Bjarki says, "See ya," like he always does, and a couple weeks later I fly to Florida to stay through the New Year beneath the elegant palm trees that do not contain any wood in another attempt, I suppose, to finally get some real separation from some things.

Acknowledgments

This book couldn't have been written without the generosity of all those people in and around The Wood Mill of Maine. Thank you to Bjarki Gunnarsson, for his friendship, his endurance, and for being himself always. Thank you to Nate Lesperance, for his patience, his knowledge, and his sense of humor. Thank you also to Myke, Sue, Don, Ethan, Menno, Bob, Hunter, Travis, Joe, Tom, Elizabeth, Robbie, Sybille, Emerald, Eugenio, and Josh.

For reading versions of this book, I am grateful to Max Garcia Conover, Eufrey Domingo, Jeremy Eichler, John Rayburn, and my sister, Kate. I am especially grateful to Jason Burge for his creative insight and moral support. Thank you to Bern Esposito, for all that she has given to me. And thank you to my brother, Sam, who has, often at a moment's notice, read more drafts of this book than I can count.

I am also grateful to Morse and Doak Builders, not only for teaching and inspiring me but for giving me the time off to write and research this book. Thank you to MacDowell and to the Maine Arts Commission, for their generous support. Thank you to John and Dotty, for a place to stay. Thank you to Ricki K, for her understanding of the moon. Thank you to the Blue Door, Gelato Fiasco, Little Dog, and Tandem Coffee, for the sugar, the caffeine, and the background hum. Thank you to Jim McCoy, for knowing it when he saw it. Thank you to Ben, Brad, George, John, John, Joy, and Walt, for guiding me in spirit. And thank you to my parents, for their radness and love.